# PROPOSALS THAT WORK

## A guide for planning research

# PROPOSALS THAT WORK

## A guide for planning research

LAWRENCE F. LOCKE
*The University of Massachusetts*

WANEEN WYRICK SPIRDUSO
*The University of Texas at Austin*

*Foreword by G. Lawrence Rarick*

TEACHERS COLLEGE PRESS
Teachers College, Columbia University
New York and London

Copyright © 1976 by Teachers College, Columbia University
Library of Congress Catalog Card Number: 76-4965

Library of Congress Cataloging in Publication Data:

Locke, Lawrence F.
Proposals that work.

Bibliography: p.
1. Research. 2. Physical education and training —
Research — Case studies. 3. Educational research.
I. Spirduso, Waneen Wyrick, joint author. II. Title.
AZ105.L54        001.4'3        76-4965
ISBN 0-8077-2495-5

Designed by Angela Foote
Manufactured in the United States of America

*For W.R. Morford, whose choleric disposition, impeccable view of scholarship, and quiet kindness so leavened our happy triangle,*

*And for W. Kroll, who has been patient mentor to us both and who, like Tadeus Kosciuszko before him, has cast his lot with a young enterprise that has great need but small capacity to repay his excellent service,*

*We gratefully and affectionately dedicate this book.*

*LFL*
*WWS*

# Foreword

$\text{T}$he preparation of a well designed research proposal is a creative and intellectually demanding task, an exercise in logic built upon the foundations of the scientific method. It is a task that most graduate students face, one that many are ill-equipped to deal with effectively, and one that all too often becomes a frustrating and emotionally traumatic experience. This is not surprising, for the primary thrust of under-graduate education is focused on the acquisition of knowledge with only limited emphasis on the development of those insights and analytical abilities needed for the design and conduct of successful research. Thus, the first-year graduate student is likely to embark on the research assignment totally naive to the demands of the task, dependent in a large measure on what can be gleaned from a one-term course in research methodology, a course that may be more confusing than enlightening. This volume should do much to alleviate this problem, for it is written from the point of view that most graduate students have neither the wisdom, the experience, nor the intuitive judgment to anticipate the many complexities that arise in the conduct of research, those difficulties that might have been anticipated and circumscribed by careful planning.

As the title implies, the book is a guide for the preparation of research proposals. It does not pretend to tell the reader how to do research, although the problems the student faces, if proper precautions are not taken in the planning stage, are clearly evident throughout.

The approach used by the writers is unique and highly effective, one that provides concrete illustrations of the weaknesses that are so often found in research proposals. The first two parts of the book point out in a clear and meaningful way exactly what a research proposal should do, how it is developed, and some of the problems that emerge in the planning and writing phases.

The twenty steps proposed by the authors in the development of the proposal provide the student with an excellent sequential plan of action. The rationale for this procedure is clearly spelled out at each step, carrying the student systematically from the "browsing, conversing, thinking stage," to the formulation of clear concise questions, to the final revised proposal. The authors effectively build on this procedure by proposing at points along the way a series of questions that might well be asked in determining if the proposed plan of action is appropriate, or if alternatives would be better.

Part III of the book should be particularly helpful to students, for here three specimen proposals are systematically dissected, with illuminating comments by the authors appropriately inserted. What makes this approach particularly effective is that the three specimen proposals are in fact the unabridged working documents of three graduate students. The authors take the reader through each proposal section by section and paragraph by paragraph, pointing out where there are ambiguities, elements of faulty logic, and materials of doubtful relevance. These critiques should give the student a clear concept of what constitutes a good review of the literature and how the review can be used as a knowledge base for the formulation of hypotheses. This procedure further illustrates how a weak research design can be strengthened and how inadequate methodologies can be improved.

Throughout the book, stress is placed on clear communication, a talent characteristic of all too few graduate students. As the authors point out, the most immediate object of the proposal is to give the reader the necessary information as quickly and as accurately as possible. Specific illustrations of how this can be done are effectively given in the critiques.

This volume is an unusually fine addition to the many published works on research methodology. Its unique approach should make the student aware of what constitutes a good proposal and the specific considerations that must be kept in mind if the proposal is to bear close scrutiny. For faculty advisers, it will be a valuable teaching aid, and for students, it will be a helpful guide.

G. Lawrence Rarick
University of California, Berkeley

# Preface

This guide contains no direct instruction concerning how to do research. Rather, the material herein deals with the problem of how to write a research proposal. Although the two capacities — skill in conducting research and skill in writing about that research — have a close relationship, they are far from coterminous. Students who have acquired considerable information and even experience in the mysteries of research design and statistics do not always know how to undertake the task of planning and effectively proposing their own investigations.

Although few students recognize it at the start, preparing the proposal represents the major hurdle in gaining approval for their theses or dissertations. No magic formula can make writing the proposal an easy task. Hopefully, however, this guide can serve to reduce both the perceived and the real dimensions of the hurdle.

David Krathwohl's (1966) description of the vision held by many young novices in research seems, in the authors' experience at least, to be quite accurate: "The adolescent envisions the researcher as one who dreams up creative ideas, the needed resources miraculously appear, and the hero, in a state of eager anticipation, begins his investigation" (p. 3).

The experienced research worker would add a number of less romantic steps to the vision of Krathwohl's novice: the agonies of finding the "miraculous" resources, the frequent tedium of collecting data, the hours of searching for background references that seem always to have been lost from the library's collection or made victim of the razor blade, and the ultimate frustration of dealing, at the end of it all, with an unsympathetic committee.

Certainly all researchers would concur in identifying the most critical omission in the novice's vision as the absence of any reference to preparing the proposal. Along with the interpretation of data and the preparation of the final report, development of the proposal constitutes the genuinely creative element in the research process. Creating the plan for research is one fountainhead of the essential fascination that keeps talented men and women at a task more often characterized by frustration and tedium than by romance and excitement.

Conducting research, in the sense of carrying out the plan for investigation, may be hard work, but in the end it demands far less intellectual ability and yields, in itself, far less satisfaction than the process of developing the proposal. The tongue-in-cheek maxim that holds the planning of research and the interpretation of data to be the proper business of the scholar, whereas the actual conduct of investigation is held to be the proper business of graduate assistants, may be somewhat overstated, but it reflects a genuine truth about the day-to-day reality of research.

The importance of the student's first formal proposal is measured by the fact that in most instances the decision to permit the student to embark on a thesis or dissertation is made solely on the basis of that document. The quality of the writing in the proposal is likely to be used by advisors as a basis for judging the clarity of thought that has preceded the study, the degree of facility with which it will be implemented if approved, and the skill of presentation the student will bring to reporting the results. In sum, the proposal is a document in which the student will reveal whether there is a reasonable hope that he can conduct any research project at all. With this much hanging in the balance, it is obvious that the proposal demands the best creative effort of the student and the most careful critical appraisal of the advisor.

Some readers may feel that the explanatory material contained in this guide is slanted toward the experimental forms of investigation. To the degree that this is true, such a bias reflects what the authors perceive to be the demands the student is likely to encounter in university and departmental requirements for proposal format. Much that can be said about experimental studies can easily be adapted to other kinds of investigation. For this reason, writing about the problems of proposing an experimental study becomes an economical and, thus, compelling convenience. As an aid to the proposer interested in other kinds of studies, the specimen proposals selected for critical appraisal in the third section of this guide contain a wide variety of methodological approaches to research.

Finally, from time to time, the reader may feel that the authors have attempted to enter into a kind of "collusion" with the student for the purpose of outwitting the research advisor. The realities of university life, with which both students and research advisors are painfully familiar, make such a position difficult to avoid. Nothing, however, could be further from the authors' actual intention. If the student-advisor relationship resembles a contest, there is small chance that reference to a guide for proposal writing will be of any real assistance.

Our purpose from start to finish has been to assist in achieving one end — a fair and useful hearing for the student's proposed study. If the proposal is rejected, it should be because it lacks genuine merit or feasibility, not because it is poorly prepared.

# Suggestions for Using the Guide

The student who is inexperienced in writing proposals will find it useful to begin with Part I, which deals with the basic functions of the proposal. He can then turn to Part III, which presents specimen examples of proposals, and select one to read through quickly, noting how the basic functions are performed in an actual proposal. He can then return to the remaining general discussion of construction and format with some appreciation of the proposal task that is based on a concrete illustration.

Turning next to Appendix A, which contains a list of standards for judging the acceptability of a proposal, the student should study and digest this section. At this point he can return to the specimen proposals and employ the list of standards in actually judging or rating one of the proposals. Thus the student can assure himself that he has grasped the major elements in preparing a sound proposal.

If he finds that he is unsure about applying any particular standard, the student may refer back to the corresponding portion of the general discussion section. He may also refer to one of the more extensive references selected from Appendix B, which contains an annotated bibliography of supplementary materials.

Finally, before embarking on the construction of his own proposal, the student should scan the section on special problems. Familiarity with the items contained in this group of commonly encountered problems can both forewarn and forearm the novice researcher, saving time and directing his attention to some of the more critical questions he must confront.

# CONTENTS

Foreword by *G. Lawrence Rarick*    vii

Preface    ix

Suggestions for Using the Guide    xiii


## PART 1
### THE FUNCTION OF THE PROPOSAL    1

Function    1
Regulations Governing Proposals    2
General Considerations    3
General Format    4
Specific Tasks    5
    *Task 1. Introducing the problem    5*
    *Task 2. Stating the problem    5*
    *Task 3. Discussing the background of the problem    5*
    *Task 4. Formulating questions or hypotheses    7*
    *Task 5. Explaining procedures    8*
    *Task 6. Providing supplementary material    9*

## PART II
## DEVELOPING THE PROPOSAL:
## SOME COMMON PROBLEMS                          11

Section 1. The Sequence of Proposing: From Selecting a
        Topic to Oral Presentation    12
    *A plan of action. . . what follows what?    12*
    *Originality and replication. . .what is a contribution
        to knowledge?    18*
    *Getting started. . . putting pen to paper    20*
    *Prologue to action. . . the oral presentation    21*
Section 2. Style and Form in Writing the Proposal    24
    *Praising, exhorting, and polemicising. . . don't    24*
    *Quotations. . . how to pick fruit from the knowledge tree    24*
    *Clarity and precision. . . speaking in system language    25*
    *Editing. . . the care and nurture of a document    28*
    *In search of a title. . . first impressions and the route
        to retrieval    29*
Section 3. Content of the Proposal: Important Considerations    32
    *Spadework. . . the proper use of pilot studies    32*
    *Murphy's Law. . . expect the unexpected    33*
    *Anticipating the analysis. . . do it now    33*
    *The statistical well. . . drinking the greatest draught    35*
    *Informed consent. . . the protection of human subjects    38*
    *The scientific state of mind. . . proof, truth, and ration-
        alized choices    40*

References    43

## PART III
## SPECIMEN PROPOSALS                             45

Proposal Number 1 — Pain Tolerance under Distracted and
        Non-Distracted Conditions in Female Athletes and
        Nonathletes    47
Proposal Number 2 — Effect of a Children's Developmental
        Clinic on Improving Selected Perceptual-Motor
        Activities    139
Proposal Number 3 — The Maccabiah Games: A Nationalistic
        Endeavor    179

# APPENDICES 217

Appendix A — Some General Standards for Judging the
   Acceptability of a Thesis or Dissertation Proposal    217
Appendix B — Annotated Bibliography of Supplementary
   References    223
Appendix C — Standards for the Use of Human Subjects and
   Specimen Form for Informed Consent    235

# PART I

# The Function
# of the Proposal

$A$ research proposal sets forth both the exact nature of the matter to be investigated and a detailed account of the methods to be employed. In addition, the proposal usually contains material supporting the importance of the topic selected and the appropriateness of the research methods to be employed.

## FUNCTION

A research proposal may serve at least three functions:

1. *Communication.* The proposal serves to communicate the student's research plans to those who give consultation and advice. The proposal is the primary resource upon which the thesis or dissertation committee must base the functions of consultation, advice, and, ultimately, consent. Both the quality of assistance obtained and the economy of consultation depend directly upon the clarity and thoroughness of the proposal.
2. *Plan.* The proposal serves as a plan for action. All empirical research consists of careful, systematic, and preplanned observations of some

restricted set of phenomena. The acceptability of results is judged exclusively in terms of the adequacy of the methods employed in making, recording, and interpreting the planned observations. The plan for observations, with its supporting arguments and explications, is the qualitative basis on which the thesis or dissertation will be judged.

A thesis or dissertation can be no better than the plan of investigation — methodology or procedures — employed. Hence, an adequate proposal sets forth the plan in step-by-step detail. The existence of a detailed plan that incorporates the most careful anticipation of problems to be confronted and contingent courses of action is the most powerful insurance against oversight or ill-considered choices during the execution phase of the investigation. The hallmark of a good proposal is a level of thoroughness and detail sufficient to permit another investigator to replicate the study, that is, to perform the same planned observations with results not substantially different from those the author might obtain.

3. *Contract.* A completed proposal, approved for execution by the sponsoring committee, constitutes a bond of agreement between the student and his advisors. The approved proposal describes a study that, if conducted competently and completely, should provide the basis for a report that would meet all standards for acceptability. Subsequent changes, introduced either by the student or by the committee, should be made only with the full knowledge and concurrence of all parties. Substantial changes should be supported by arguments for absolute necessity or compelling desirability. In all but rare instances, revision of the proposal should be completed prior to the collection of data.

## REGULATIONS GOVERNING PROPOSALS

No set of universal rules or guidelines presently exists to govern the form or content of the research proposal. There are, however, several sources of regulations governing the form and content of the final research report. Inasmuch as the proposal sets forth a plan of action that must eventuate in a report conforming to these latter regulations, it is important to consider them in writing the proposal.

Although it is evident that particular traditions have evolved within individual departments of physical education, it is rare to find the imposition of any formal limitation on the selection of either topic or method of investigation. What normally circumscribes the planning and execution of student research are existing departmental policy on format for the final report, university regulations concerning theses and dissertation reports, and informal standards exercised by individual advisors or study committees.

In most cases, departmental and university regulations are either so explicit as to be perfectly clear (examples: "The proposal may not exceed 25 typewritten pages" or "The proposal will conform to the style established in W. C. Campbell, *Form and Style in Thesis Writing"*) or so general as to impose no specific or useful standard (examples: "The research topic must be of suitable proportions" or "The proposal must reflect a thorough knowledge of the problem area"). The student, therefore, should find no serious difficulty in developing a proposal that conforms to departmental and university regulations.

The third potential source of regulation, the individual thesis or dissertation committee, does constitute an important variable in the department of a proposal. Individuals serving on the sponsoring committee may have strong personal commitments concerning particular working procedures, writing styles, and proposal format. The student must confront these as a unique constellation of demands that will influence the form of his proposal. It always is wise to anticipate conflicting demands and to attempt their resolution before the collection of data and the preparation of a final report.

Committees are unlikely to make style and format demands that differ substantially from commonly accepted modes of research writing. As a general rule, most advisors subscribe to the broad guidelines outlined in this document. Where differences occur, they are likely to be matters of emphasis or largely mechanical items (example: inclusion of particular sub-headings within the document).

## GENERAL CONSIDERATIONS

Most problems in preparing a proposal are straightforward and relatively obvious. The common difficulties do not involve the subtle and complex problems of design and data management. They arise instead from the most basic elements of the research process: What is the proper question to ask? Where is the best place to look for the answer? How best to standardize, quantify, and record observations? Determining the answers to these questions remains the most common obstacle to the development of adequate proposals.

Simplicity, clarity, and parsimony are the standards of writing that reflect adequate thinking about the research problem. A proposal helps the student solicit prompt and accurate advice to the degree that the document is easily and correctly understood by his advisors. Complicated matters are best communicated when they are the clear objects of terse, well-edited prose. In the mass of details and intellectual efforts that go into the planning of a research study, the student must not forget that the proposal's most immediate function is to inform his readers quickly and accurately.

The problem in writing a proposal is essentially the same as in writing the final report. When the task of preparing a proposal is well executed, the task of preparing the final report is more than half done. Under ideal conditions, such minor changes as altering the tense of verbs converts the proposal into the opening chapters of the final report.

Most, although not necessarily all, proposals evolve through a series of steps from preliminary discussions with colleagues and faculty members to a final document presented at a formal meeting of the full dissertation or thesis committee. This process can be accelerated and made more productive if the student follows these simple rules:

1. Prepare clean, updated copies of the evolving proposal and submit them to advisors in advance of scheduled consultations.
2. Prepare agenda of questions and problems to be discussed and submit them to advisors in advance of scheduled consultations.
3. Keep a carefully written record of the discussion and decisions that occur with regard to each item on the consultation agendum.

A number of research textbooks and form guides are available to help in developing an adequate proposal. In addition, checklists now exist for reviewing the adequacy of proposals for several specific types of research. Appendix B contains a list of such material.

The most useful single document for many students may be Davitz and Davitz, *A Guide for Evaluating Research Plans in Psychology and Education* (Teachers College Press, 1967). This short treatise should be read and reread before actual work on the proposal begins. The checklist of questions provided by Davitz and Davitz should be applied and specific answers noted at each new stage of the proposal's development.

A list of general standards for judging the acceptability of a thesis or dissertation proposal is given in Appendix A. This list can serve both as a preliminary guide for anticipating problems in development of the proposal and as a checklist to use in revising and refining the final document.

## GENERAL FORMAT

Guidelines for the format of proposals, even when intended only as general suggestions, often have an unfortunate influence on the writing process. Once committed to paper, such guidelines quickly tend to acquire the status of mandatory prescription. In an attempt to conform to what they perceive as an invariate format, students produce proposal documents that are awkward and illogical as plans for action, as well as stilted and tasteless as prose writing.

*There is no universally applicable and correct format for the research proposal.* Nonetheless, there are certain communication tasks to be accomplished. A few of these tasks are common to all proposals, whereas other tasks are unique to particular research topics. Taken together, the tasks encompassed by the proposal demand the creation of a format designed to fit the real topic at hand, not some preconceived ideal.

## SPECIFIC TASKS

The following paragraphs specify communication tasks that are present in nearly all proposals for empirical research. Within a given proposal the tasks may or may not be identified by such traditional section designations as "Background," "Importance," "Review of Literature," "Methodology," "Definitions," or "Limitations." Particular proposals are sure to demand changes in the order of presentation or attention to yet other tasks not specified below. It is particularly important to note that adjacent tasks in the following paragraphs often may be conveniently merged into single sections.

### Task 1. Introducing the problem

Proposals, like other forms of written communications, are best introduced by a short, meticulously devised statement that establishes the overall area of concern, arouses interest, and communicates information essential to the reader's comprehension of what follows. The standard here is "gentle introduction" that avoids both tedious length and the shock of technical detail or abstruse argument. A careful and artful introductory statement is the precursor of *Task 3* (Background) and may, in fact, simply be written as the opening portion of that later task.

### Task 2. Stating the problem

Early in the proposal it is wise to set forth an explicit statement of the problem to which the investigation will be directed. The statement of problem need not include all sub-problems, nor need it be stated in the formal language of research questions or hypotheses. It should, however, provide a specific and accurate synopsis of the overall purpose of the study. An early and specific announcement of the research problem satisfies the most pressing of the reader's needs. Such information leaves the reader free to attend to the author's subsequent exposition and development of the topic without the nagging sense of having to hunt for the main object of study. Consequently, it is useful to give the statement of the problem high visibility.

### Task 3. Discussing the background of the problem

Any research problem must show its lineage from the background of existing knowledge, previous investigation, or, in the case of applied research, from contemporary practice. The author must answer three questions:

1. What do we already know or do? (The purpose here is to support the legitimacy and importance of the question.)
2. How does this particular question relate to what we already know or do? (The purpose here is to explain and support the exact form of questions or hypotheses that serve as the focus for the study.)
3. Why select this particular method of investigation? (The purpose here is to explain and support the selections made from among alternative methods of investigation.)

In reviewing the research literature that often forms the background for the study, the author's task is to indicate the main directions taken by workers in the area and the main issues of methodology and interpretation that have arisen. Particular attention must be given to a critical analysis of previous methodology and the exposition of the advantages and limitations inherent in various alternatives. Close attention must be given to conceptual and theoretical formulations that are explicit or implicit within the selected studies.

By making the selection of method contingent upon previous results, by making the questions or hypotheses emerge from the total matrix of answered and unanswered questions, by devising, when appropriate, a theoretical basis for the study that emerges from the structure of existing knowledge, the author inserts his proposed study into a line of inquiry and a developing body of knowledge. Such careful attention to background is the first step in entering the continuing conversation that is science.

The author should select only those studies that provide a foundation for the proposed investigation, discuss these studies in sufficient detail to make their relevance entirely clear, note explicitly the ways in which they contribute to the proposed research, and give some indication of how the proposal is designed to move beyond earlier work.

It is important for the student to resist the impulse to display both the extent of his personal labors in achieving what he knows and the volume of interesting but presently irrelevant information he has accumulated in the process. The rule in selecting studies for review is exactly the same as that used throughout the proposal — limit discussion to what is essential to the main topic. A complete list of all references used in developing the proposal — properly called a bibliography as distinct from the list of references — may be placed in the appendix, thereby providing both a service to the interested reader and some psychological relief to the student.

Whenever possible, the author should provide conceptual or theoretical clarity by creating organizing frameworks that encompass both the reviewed studies and the proposed research. This may take the form of something as obvious and practical as grouping studies according to certain methodological features (often for the purpose of examining divergent results), or something as esoteric as identifying and grouping the implicit assumptions made by various researchers in formulating their statement of the problem (often for the purpose of clarifying the problem elected in the present proposal).

In many proposals, the creation of an organizing framework represents the most important single opportunity for the application of original thought. In one sense, the organizing task is an extension of the need to achieve clarity in communication. A category system that allows division of diverse ideas or recondite events into easily perceived and remembered subsets is an organizational convenience for the author, as well as for the reader. Beyond convenience, however, the development of organizing frameworks involves identifying distinctive threads of thought. The task here is to isolate the common ways by which researchers, working at different times and in varying degrees of intellectual isolation, have conceived of reality. In creating a schema that deals meaningfully with similarities and dissimilarities in the work of other men, the author of the proposal can serve both his own needs and the developing body of knowledge.

Even relatively simple organizing or integrating systems demand the development of underlying conceptual plans and, often, new ways of interpreting old results and presumed relationships. The sequence of variables in the study may provide a simple and generally adequate place to begin arranging the review. Such questions as "What is the relationship between social class and achievement in physical education when ability is held as a constant?" consist of concepts placed within a convenient sequential diagram. In turn, such conceptual schemata often contain useful assumptions about causal relationships and thus can serve as effective precursors to explanatory theory. The most elegant kind of research proposals achieve exactly that kind of linkage, using the framework for organizing the review of literature as a bridge connecting existing knowledge, a proposed theory, and the specific, theory-based hypotheses to be given empirical test in the proposed study.

## Task 4. Formulating questions or hypotheses

All proposals must arrive at a formal statement of questions or hypotheses. These may be set aside as a separate section or simply included in the course of other discussion. Such statements differ from the earlier statement of the problem in that (1) they are normally stated in formal terms appropriate to the design and analysis of data to be employed, and (2) they display, in logical order, all sub-parts of the problem.

The question form is most appropriate where the research is exploratory. The researcher should indicate by the specificity of questions, however, how carefully he has thought through the problem. By careful formulation of questions, the proposed study should be directed toward suspected alternatives rather than toward a scanning of "interesting" findings.

Hypotheses must be related to a theoretical base and should be employed whenever the state of existing knowledge permits the formulation of intelligent suppositions about the relationship of elements in the problematic area. Even if the theoretical framework has been introduced in a previous section, it often is useful to provide a succinct restatement at a point contiguous to the formal presentation of hypotheses.

The proposal must provide a clear bridge connecting knowledge, theory, and the proposed study. The process of translating the relationships expressed in theory into the form of testable hypotheses involves logical operations that will be critical to the reader's understanding. For that reason, the author must make every effort to present a clear account of how he moves from knowledge to theory to hypotheses to methodology.

## Task 5.  Explaining procedures

All proposals for empirical research must embody a plan for the careful and systematic observation of events. The methods selected for such observations determine the quality of data obtained. For this reason, the portion of the proposal dealing with procedures the researcher intends to employ will be subject to the closest critical scrutiny. Correspondingly, the presentation of methodology requires great attention to detail. The discussion of method must include sources of data, the collection of data, and the analysis of data. In addition, the discussion must show that the specific techniques selected will not fall short of the claims established in previous sections of the proposal.

The section or sections dealing with methodology must be freely adapted to the purpose of the study. Whatever the format, however, the proposal must provide a step-by-step set of instructions for conducting the investigation. For example, many studies demand explication of the following items:

1.  Identification and description of the target population and sampling methods to be used.
2.  Presentation of instruments and techniques for measurement.
3.  Presentation of a design for the collection of data.
4.  Presentation of procedures for collecting and recording data.
5.  Development of plans for such contingencies as subject mortality.
6.  Presentation of plans for the analysis of data.

Many of the justifications for particular selections of method will emerge in the development of background for the problem. The rationale for some choices, however, will most conveniently be presented when the method is introduced as part of the plan for investigation.

## Task 6. Providing supplementary material

For the purpose of clarity and economical presentation, many items may be placed in appendices keyed to appropriate references in the main text. So placed, such materials become options available to the reader as needed, rather than distractions or impediments to understanding the main themes of the proposal. Included in the appendices may be such items as the following:

1.  Specifications for equipment.
2.  Instructions to subjects.
3.  Letters and other relevant documents.
4.  Subject consent forms.
5.  Raw data or tabular material from pilot studies.
6.  Copies of verbal instruments.
7.  Interview schedules.
8.  Credentials of experts, judges, or other special personnel to be employed in the study.
9.  Diagrammatic models of the research design.
10. Diagrammatic models of the statistical analysis.
11. Tabular materials from related research.
12. Chapter outline for the final report.
13. Proposed time schedule for executing the study.
14. Supplementary bibliographies.

# PART II

## Developing
## the Proposal:
## Some Common Problems

The general purposes and broad format of the proposal document have now been presented. There remain, however, a number of particular points that cause a disproportionate amount of difficulty in preparing proposals for student-conducted research.

In some cases the problems arise because of real difficulty in the subtle and complex nature of the writing task. In other cases, however, the problems are a consequence of confusion, conflicting opinions, and ambiguous standards among research workers themselves and, more particularly, among university research advisors.

As with many tasks involving an element of art, it is possible to establish a few general rules to which most practitioners subscribe. Success in terms of real mastery, however, lies not in knowing or even following the rules, but in what the student learns to do within the rules.

Each student will discover his own set of special problems. Some will be solved only through practice and the accumulation of experience. While wrestling with the frustrations of his proposal, the student should remind himself that the fascination of research lies in its problematic nature, in the tortuous search for more serviceable hypotheses, in the creative tasks of design, and in the stringent demand for clear, concise expression.

The services that can be provided here are to warn the student about the most common pitfalls, to provide some general suggestions for resolution of the problems, and to sound one encouraging note: Consultation with colleagues and advisors, patience with the often slow process of "figuring out," and scrupulous care in writing will overcome or circumvent most of the problems encountered in preparing a research proposal. In the midst of difficulty, it is useful to remember that problems are better encountered when developing the proposal than when facing a deadline for the final copy of the thesis.

The problems have been grouped into three broad categories: Section 1. The Sequence of Proposing: From Selecting a Topic to Oral Presentation; Section 2. Style and Form in Writing the Proposal; and Section 3. Content of the Proposal: Important Considerations. Each section contains a number of specific issues that may confront the student researcher, and provides some rules of thumb for use in avoiding or resolving the attendant difficulties. Students should skim through the three sections and read selectively, since not all of the discussions will be relevant to their needs.

## SECTION 1. THE SEQUENCE OF PROPOSING: FROM SELECTING A TOPIC TO ORAL PRESENTATION

**A plan of action . . . what follows what?** The diagram on pages 14-15 can be useful for the novice if one central point is understood. A tidy, linear sequence of steps is *not* an accurate picture of what happens in the development of most research proposals. The peculiar qualities of human thought processes and the serendipity of retrieving knowledge serve to guarantee that development of a proposal will be anything but tidy. Dizzying leaps, periods of no progress, and agonizing backtracking are more typical than is a continuous, unidirectional flow of events. The diagram may be used to obtain an overview of the task, to establish a rough time schedule, or to check retrospectively for possible omissions, but it is not to be taken as a literal representation of what should or will happen.*

To say that development of a proposal is not a perfectly predictable sequence is not to say, however, that it is entirely devoid of order. When the proposal has been completed, a backward glance often indicates that an orderly progression through the steps would have saved time and effort. It is more important to complete some steps in sequence than others. For instance, although the mind may skip ahead and visualize a specific type of measure to be used, Step (11) "Consider alternative methods of measurement"

---

*Boxes represent major procedural steps; unbroken lines trace the main sequence of those steps. Circles represent the major questions to be confronted; the broken lines lead to the procedural consequences of the alternative (YES) or (NO) answers.

should not be undertaken until Step (6) "Surveying relevant literature" is completed. Many methods of measurement may be revealed and noted while perusing the literature. Sometimes suggestions for instrumentation materialize in unlikely places, or in studies that have been placed by the student into categories that seem unlikely to yield information concerning measurement. In addition, reported reliabilities and validities of alternative procedures will be needed before any final selection can be made. Thus, a large commitment of effort to consideration of alternative methods can be a waste of time if it precedes a careful survey of the literature.

For simplicity, many important elements have been omitted from the diagram. No reference is made to such pivotal processes as developing a theoretical framework, categorizing literature, or stating hypotheses. Further, the detailed demands that are intrinsic to the writing process itself, such as establishing a systematic language, receive no mention. What is presented are the obvious steps of logic and procedure — the operations and questions that mark development toward a plan for action. The following points within the diagram are the most frequent causes of difficulty.

*Step 3. Narrow down. What do I want to know?* Moving from general to specific is always more difficult for the beginner than he anticipates. It is here that the student has his first encounter with two of the hard facts of scientific life: logistic practicality and the perverse inscrutability of seemingly simple events. Inevitably, he must learn to take one small step, one manageable question, at a time. In other words, the proposal must conform in scope to the realistic limitations of the research process itself. At their best, the tools of research can encompass only limited bits of reality, and, stretched too far, they produce illusion rather than understanding.

It is important to think big at first, to puzzle without considering practicality, and to allow speculation to soar beyond the confines of the sure knowledge base. From such creative conceptual exercises, however, the researcher must return to the question, "Where, given my resources and the nature of the problem, can I begin?"

Delimiting questions such as "In which people?" "Under what conditions?" "At what time?" "In what location?" "By observing which events?" "By manipulating which variables?" serve the necessary pruning function.

*Question A. Still worth pursuing?* A question's worth may be viewed from two dimensions: that of its worth to the individual contemplating the answer, and that of its worth to the profession, to the academic community, and ultimately to society. Question A, "Still worth pursuing?," is the question that the researcher must answer in terms of his own interests and needs. The world is full of clearly formulated and specific questions that may not, once seen in their formal dress, seem worth the effort of answering. Because researchers are human, perfectly legitimate questions may seem dull, interesting veins of inquiry may peter out into triviality, and well-defined issues may fail to suit for no better reason than a clash with personal style. On the other

## Twenty Steps to a Proposal

*Begin here.*

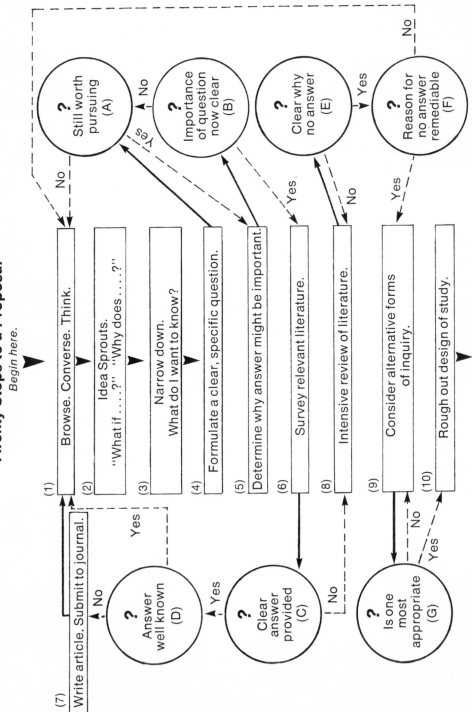

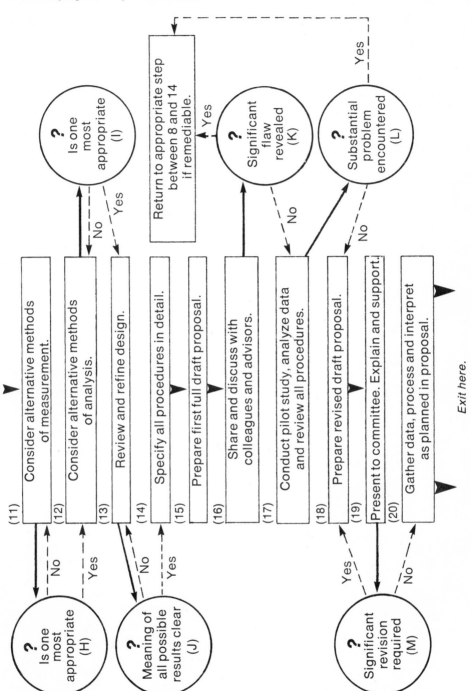

hand, some questions are supported by the researcher's immediate needs to enhance his teaching in a vital subject area or to quench his curiosity about a long-held hunch.

The basic rule is to be honest before proceeding. If you really don't care about answering the question, it may be better to start again, while the investment still is relatively small.

*Step 5. Determine why it might be important to answer.* This step places the proposed research in scientific-societal perspective. The study should contribute to the generation or validation of a theoretical structure or subcomponent, or relate to one of the several processes by which knowledge is used to enhance professional practice. The trick here is to justify the question in terms appropriate to the nature of the question. Inquiry that is directed toward filling a gap in the structure of knowledge need not be supported by appeals to practical application (even though later events may yield just such return). Inquiry that arises directly from problems in the world of practice need not be supported by appeals to improve understanding of basic phenomena (even though later events may yield just such return). Each kind of question has its own correct measure of importance. The task of distinguishing the trivial from the substantive is not always easy; do not make it even more difficult by attempting to apply the wrong standard.

*Step 6. Survey relevant literature.* A preliminary scanning of the most obvious, pertinent resources, particularly reviews of the literature, is a way of husbanding time. It is far better to abandon a line of thought after several weeks of selective skimming than to work one's way via slow, thorough digestion of each document to the same conclusion after several months of effort.

Conscientious students sometimes feel vaguely guilty about such quick surveys. Keeping in mind the real purpose, which is to identify questions that already have satisfactory answers, is one way of easing such discomfort.

*Question F. Reason for missing answer remediable?* In some cases the literature contains an empty area because the state of technology, the available knowledge framework, or the logistic demands peculiar to the question have made it impossible or unreasonable to conduct appropriate forms of inquiry. So long as the gap in knowledge seems to exist because no one has yet defined the question or become interested in pursuing the answer, it is reasonable to proceed. There are other reasons for empty or ambiguous areas in the literature, however, and they signal caution before proceeding.

*Question J. Meaning of all possible results clear?* The tighter the logic, the more elegant the theoretical framework, the more closely the design is tailored to produce clarity along one dimension, in short, the better the quality of the proposal, the greater the risk that the proposer will be lured into an unfortunate presumption — that he knows the result of his study before the data are in hand.

That student researchers sometimes are confronted by the stunning news that their treatment produced a reverse effect is in itself neither surprising nor harmful. Being unable to make an intelligent interpretation of such a situation is, however, unfortunate and in some cases unnecessary.

By serious consideration of every possible result at the time of constructing the proposal, it often becomes possible to include elements in the study that will give substance to any of several possible results. One method of anticipating the unexpected is to follow through the consequences of rejecting or failing to reject each hypothesis of the study. If the hypothesis were to be rejected, what is the explanation? How is the explanation justified by the rationale for the study? What findings would support the explanation? Conversely, if the findings of the study fail to provide a basis for rejection, what explanations are to be proposed? What are alternative explanations? At the least, some careful preliminary thought about alternative explanations for each possible result will serve as a shield against the panic that produces such awkward *post hoc* interpretations as "no significant differences were observed because the instruments employed were inadequate."

*Step 16. Share and discuss with colleagues and advisors.* There is a well-known syndrome displayed by some who attempt research, symptomized by the inclination to prolong the period of writing the final report — indefinitely. Some people simply cannot face what they perceive to be the personal threat implied in opening their work to challenge in the public arena. These individuals are terribly handicapped and only rarely can become mature, productive scientists. An early sign of this syndrome is seen in students who cannot bring themselves to solicit advice and criticism for their proposals.

Sometimes a student experiences severe criticism because he presents his ideas before they have been sufficiently developed into a conceptual framework that represents careful and critical preparation. Many professors avoid specualtive conversations about "half-baked" ideas that have just arrived in a blinding flash of revelation to the student. Few professors refuse a request for advice concerning a proposal that has been drafted as the culmination of several weeks of hard thought, research, and development. Even at that, having one's best effort devastated by pointed criticism can be an agonizing experience. The only alternative, however, is to persist in error or ignorance, and that is untenable in research.

If the student is fortunate enough to be in a department that contains a vigorous community of inquiring minds, with the constant give and take of intellectual disputation, he soon will learn to regard the rough and tumble as a functional part of producing good research. He will solicit, if not enjoy, the best criticism he can find.

The notion that it is vaguely immoral to seek assistance in preparing a proposal is at best a parody of real science and at worst, as in the form of an institutional rule, it is a serious perversion arising from ignorance. Research may have some game-like qualities, but a system of handicaps is not one of them. The object of every inquiry is to get the best possible answer under the circumstances, and that presumes obtaining the best advice available. Hopefully, the student will not be held to any lesser standard.

It should be obvious that the student, after digesting and weighing all the criticism he receives, must still make his own choices. Not all advice is good and not all criticism is valid. There is only one way to find out, however, and that is to share the proposal with colleagues whose judgments one can respect, if not always accept.

*Step 20.  Gather data, process, and interpret as in proposal.*  This is the pay-off. A good proposal is more than a guide to action, it is a framework for intelligent interpretation of results and the heart of a sound final report. The proposal cannot guarantee significant results, but it will provide some assurance that, whatever the result, the student can wind up the project with reasonable dispatch and at least a minimum of intellectual grace. If that sounds too small a recompense for all the effort, consider the alternative of having to write a report about an inconsequential question, pursued through inadequate methods of inquiry, and resulting in a heap of unanalyzable data.

**Originality and replication . . . what is a contribution to knowledge?**  In this brief monograph, the authors have not attempted to discuss events that precede the proposal, the critical and difficult steps of identifying and delimiting a research topic, but at least one such preliminary problem, the question of originality, has important ramifications for the proposal and thus must receive comment here.

Some advisors regard student-conducted research primarily as an arena for training, wood-chopping that is expected to produce muscles in the axeman but not much real fuel for the fire. Whatever may be the logic of such an assumption, it goes without saying that students generally do not take the same attitude. Their expectations are more likely to resemble the classic dictum for scholarly research, to make an original contribution to the body of knowledge.

An all-too-common problem in selecting topics for research proposals occurs when either the student or an advisor gives literal interpretation to the word "original," defining it as "initial, first, never having existed or occurred before." This is a serious misinterpretation of the word as it is used in science. In research, "original" clearly includes all studies deliberately employed to test the accuracy of results or the applicability of conclusions developed in previous studies. What are not included under the rubric of "original" are studies that proceed mindlessly to repeat an existing work either in foolish ignorance of its existence or without appropriate attention to its defects or limitations.

One consequence of the confusion surrounding the phrase "original contribution" is that misguided students and advisors are led to ignore one of the most important areas of research activity and one of the most useful forms of training for the novice researcher — replication. That replication sometimes is regarded simply as rote imitation, lacking sufficient opportunity for the student to apply and develop his own skills, is an indication of how badly some students and advisors misunderstand both the operation of a research enterprise and the concept of a body of knowledge.

The essential role of replication in research has been argued elsewhere with great cogency (Bauernfeind, 1968; Pelton, 1970). What has not been made sufficiently clear, however, is that replication can involve challenging problems that demand creative resolution. Further, as a consequence of inexperience, some advisors do not appreciate the degree to which writing proposals for replicative studies can constitute an ideal learning opportunity for research trainees.

In direct replication the student is confronted not only with correctly identifying all the critical variables in the original study, but with creating equivalent conditions for the conduct of his own study. Anyone who thinks that the critical variables will immediately be apparent from a reading of the original report has not read very widely in the research literature of physical education. Anyone who thinks that truly equivalent conditions can be created simply by "doing it the same way" just has not tried to perform a replicative study. Thorough understanding of the problem and, frequently, a great deal of technical ingenuity are demanded in developing an adequate proposal for direct replication.

As an alternative to direct replication, the student may repeat an interesting study that he considers to have been defective in sample, method, analysis, or interpretation. Here the student introduces deliberate changes to improve the power of a previous investigation. It would be difficult to imagine a more challenging or useful activity for anyone interested in both learning about research and contributing to the accumulation of reliable knowledge.

In writing a proposal for either kind of replicative study, direct or revised, the student should introduce the original with appropriate citation, make the comments that are needed, and proceed without equivocation or apology to propose his own work. Replicative research is not, as unfortunate tradition has it in some departments, slightly improper or something less than genuine research.

The cross validation study is another type of study that sometimes is characterized as unoriginal, and even sometimes is confused with replication. An excellent example of a cross validation study has been provided by Kroll and Peterson (1966). Cross validation studies most frequently appear in conjunction with or following multiple regression studies, in which the investigator attempts to determine an equation by which he can predict a dependent variable or variables. The equations that are derived for the sample used, however, are affected somewhat by chance correlations and errors of measurement, to the extent that the investigator cannot be sure how predictive the set of variables he selected would be for other samples.

Two techniques of cross validation are used. In one technique the investigator computes a predicted score for each of his subjects — on the basis of the equation derived from the original study — and then correlates his predicted scores with the scores that he actually measured in the second sample. If he obtains a very high correlation between those predicted scores and his measured scores in an entirely different sample, he has validated the original set of independent variables with their given weights as being generally predictive of the dependent variable. A second technique is to use the second sample to derive a new set of regression weights and a new multiple $R$ coefficient for the originally selected independent variables.

Another situation in which cross validation is used involves studies in which an investigator selects from a large pool of test items those that significantly discriminate between two or more groups. Again, chance plays a role in the differentiation of the groups — perhaps creating spuriously large differences, or an inflated correlation between the criterion and the sample upon which the selection of items was based. In studies of this type, cross validation on additional groups is required.

Irrespective of the situation in which cross validation is used, or the technique used to accomplish it, it should be readily apparent that cross validation does not require a completely original effort. Yet it is a technique sorely needed in the behavioral sciences. The pool of knowledge in most behavioral sciences would be deepened and clarified much faster if many of the thousands of theses undertaken each year were careful cross validations or replications rather than inexperienced and misguided attempts at originality.

Given the limitations of research reports, it often is useful to discuss the source study for the replication or cross validation with the original author, directly or by mail. Most research workers are happy to provide greater detail and in some instances raw data for inspection or reanalysis. In a healthy science, replication is the most sincere form of flattery.

A proposal appendix containing correspondence with the author of the original report, or data not provided in that report, can often serve to interest and reassure a hesitant advisor.

**Getting started . . . putting pen to paper.** It is quite common for the student who has never written a research proposal to sit in front of his typewriter or desk and stare at a blank piece of paper for hours. In short, his mind is brimming with knowledge gleaned from the literature, but how does he actually get it on the paper? It is true, too, that the concept of "a research proposal" conjures up ideas of accuracy, precision, meticulous form, and the use of a language system that is quite foreign to the neophyte researcher. If the student is overwhelmed by such demands, the following suggestions may be helpful.

Make an outline that is compatible with the format selected to present the communication tasks. An initial approval of the outline by the advisor may save later revision time. Gather the resource materials, notes, and references, and organize them into groups that correspond to the outline topics. For instance, notes supporting the rationale of the study would be in one group, and notes relating to the reliability of an instrument to be used would be in another group.

Once the outline is made and the materials gathered, tackle one of the topics in the outline (preferably the first) and start writing. If the topic to be written is labeled "The Problem," assume someone has asked the question, "What is the problem of this study?" Your task is to answer that question. Start writing. Do not worry about grammar, syntax, or writing within the language system. Just write. In this way you can avoid one of the greatest inhibitions to creativity — an inward criticism that is so severe that each idea is rejected before it becomes reality. Remember, it is easier to correct than to create. If all the essential parts of a topic are displayed in some fashion, they can later be rearranged, edited, and couched within the language system. With experience, the student will find himself thinking in the language system and forms of the proposal. Until that time, the essential problem is to begin. Awkward or elegant, laborious or swift, there is no substitute for writing the first draft.

**Prologue to action . . . the oral presentation.** Many graduate schools require a formal oral presentation of research plans before the student's committee (or a special seminar group designed for screening proposals). Masters thesis committees vary in number from one professor to a committee of five or six faculty members. A dissertation committee typically consists of four to six members. In some instances, all committee members are from within the department of the student's major. In other instances, the committee is a multi-disciplinary committee, with faculty representing other departments on the campus.

In preparing for the oral presentation, the student should identify in advance the individuals who will hear his presentation, particularly as the presence of scholars from outside the student's discipline may impose special demands on both the presentation and the period of discussion and questions that normally follows. A multi-disciplinary committee certainly makes it imperative to refrain, at least in the oral summary, from technical detail or jargon specific to the area of the study.

The type of oral presentation demanded of the student will vary from committee to committee. Some committees will carefully study the proposal and not expect a verbal recitation of what has been written. Rather, they may request a brief review of the student's past experiences that led to his topic of study, some discussion of his skills and abilities within the area of his proposed research, and some commentary about his ultimate purpose in choosing the specific topic proposed. A committee of this type, having broken the ice with such general discussion, may then settle down to question the student on specific points in the proposal.

Other committees may expect the student verbally to summarize each part of the proposal, making reference to tables, lists, or diagrams as he comes to them. In this case, the student should construct an outline of the major headings of the document and be prepared to discuss each of these without reading directly from the proposal. The committee may interject questions as the student progresses through the proposal. In special cases where unusual, inventive, or particularly complex equipment is to be used, a model, diagram, or photograph of the item may be helpful.

If a suitable space is conveniently available, a five- or ten-minute demonstration of data collection may be planned. The student may have a test administrator and subject prepared to undergo data collection as soon as he and his committee enter the room. These demonstrations serve to bring committee members more quickly within the frame of reference of the student and his advisor, and their questions can then be directed exactly to equipment functioning and administrative procedures rather than toward attempts at understanding the nature of the equipment.

A third type of committee may request a five- or ten-minute summary of the proposal as a whole, the conclusion of which is followed by questions relating to any part of the proposal. It is advisable to discover, either from the chairman or from conferences with committee members, the type of presentation they expect.

The major purpose of the oral presentation and discussion with a committee is to bring critical analysis and fresh ideas representing substantial research experience to bear upon the student's topic of study. The exposure of major flaws in design or inappropriate analyses may be discussed by the committee and the student, with the result that a solution is identified. The student should anticipate that the oral presentation is a cooperative effort toward excellence by faculty and student, and should, therefore, look forward to the experience as one that will add substantially to the probability of success in his endeavor.

The oral presentation is the time when the student's knowledge of his area of interest will serve him well. Although a large percentage of his knowledge regarding the study is not directly appropriate for insertion in the proposal, the questions of the committee and the following discussion will test the extent and depth of the student's knowledge in the area. He should, therefore, review his working notes prior to the oral presentation and have the major items of pertinent literature fresh in his memory. A thorough review of the statistical techniques involved in the proposed study will avoid confusion and possible embarrassment.

The student may be disappointed to be asked questions that reveal a committee member's failure to read the proposal carefully. In these cases it is best to answer the question briefly and then note that an attempt to answer the question can be found in the proposal on a specific page. The student should not reveal impatience with committee members who ask redundant questions; rather he should center all his attention and skill on the task of achieving complete understanding of the project by the entire committee.

It may happen that a member of the committee will press a general point of view or urge a specific decision that the student does not find compatible with his own understanding of the study. In such cases there is one useful strategy available to the student beyond the exercise of prudence, patience, and his own ability to contest the matter. If the student tries to give a thorough and lucid statement of the advisor's point in a form such as, "I believe that I understand what you are suggesting. It is that . . . ," he may find the advisor less inclined to impose his viewpoint or, at least, less inclined to press for an immediate decision. The reason for this is that most advisors are far more concerned with being understood, with being assured that the student has grasped correctly the alternative arguments upon which final decisions must be made, than with imposing their personal viewpoint on an unwilling advisee.

Another frustrating situation that may occur, although it should not be surprising to the student, is when committee members disagree among themselves on the use of a particular technique, design, or procedure. This happens quite frequently, as faculty members have strong biases regarding such matters as the statement format of hypotheses, the purpose and length of the introductory remarks, or the method of analyzing data. Generally, when serious disagreements arise, the committee eventually will come to some compromise on the issue. The student should take careful notes about the compromises reached and the preferences of each committee member. The student should make certain, before the oral presentation is terminated, that each member of the committee understands the nature and extent of the compromise that was accepted.

In preparation for the oral presentation, the student should practice before several other graduate students, presenting his work just as he intends to present to his committee, and then entertaining a substantial period of questioning. Practice in fielding questions is sound preparation for the oral. It is wise to hold a practice session before the final draft of the proposal is prepared, as questions often point to needed clarifications or revisions in the document.

## SECTION 2. STYLE AND FORM IN
## WRITING THE PROPOSAL

**Praising, exhorting, and polemicising . . . don't.** For a variety of motives arising principally from the reward system governing other writing tasks, many students use their proposal as an opportunity to praise the importance of physical activity, sports, or physical education. Some use exhortative language to urge such particular points of view as the supposed importance of empirical research in designing professional practice. Others use the proposed research as the basis for arguments suggesting such particular value decisions as the virtues of vigorous exercise.

There is no need or proper place in a research proposal for such subjective side excursions. The purpose of a proposal is to set forth for a reader the exact nature of the matter to be investigated and a detailed account of the methods to be employed. Anything else distracts and serves as an impediment to clear communication.

As a general rule, it is best to stick to the topic and resist the temptation to sound "properly positive and enthusiastic." Do not attempt to manipulate the opinions of the reader in areas other than those essential to the investigation. The simple test is to ask yourself this question, "Does the reader really need to consider this point in order to judge the adequacy of my thinking?" If the answer is "no," then the decision to delete is clear, if not always easy, for the author.

**Quotations . . . how to pick fruit from the knowledge tree.** Too often, inexperienced students are inclined to equate the number of citations in a paper with the weight of the argument being presented. This, of course, is an error. The proper purposes served by the system of scholarly citation are limited to a few specific tasks (these tasks are noted in Appendix A). When a document has all the citations needed to meet the demands of those few tasks, it has enough. When it contains more citations, it has too many and is defective in that regard.

The proper uses of direct quotation are even more stringently limited than the use of general citations for paraphrased material. The practice of liberally sprinkling the proposal with quoted material – particularly lengthy quotes – is more than pointless, it is self-defeating. The first truth is that no one will read them. The second truth is that most readers find the presence of unessential quotes irritating and a distraction from the line of thought being presented for examination. When quotations are introduced at points for which even general citations are unnecessary, the writer has reached the limit of disregard for his reader.

There are two legitimate motives for direct use of another scholar's words: (1) the weight of authoritative judgment, in which "who said it" is of critical importance, and (2) the nature of expression, in which "how it was said" is the important element. In the former instance, when unexpected, unusual, or genuinely pivotal points are to be presented, it is reasonable to show the reader that another competent craftsman has reached exactly the desired conclusion, or observed exactly the event at issue. In the latter instance, when another writer has hit upon the precise, perfect phrasing to express a difficult point, it is proper to employ his talent in behalf of your own argument. The rule to follow is simple. If the substance of a quotation can be conveyed by a careful paraphrase, followed, of course, by the appropriate credit of a citation, with all of the clarity and persuasive impact of the original, *then don't quote.*

In almost all instances it is best for the proposer to speak directly to his reader. The intervention of words from a third party should be reserved, like heavy cannon in battle, for those rare instances when the targets are specific and truly critical to the outcome of the contest.

A technique that is beneficial to the student who recognizes his own propensity toward excessive quotation is to use the critical summary form of note taking. In this format, each article or book — after careful citation — is critically examined and then paraphrased on reference cards in the student's own words. During note-taking, a decision is made on whether the aesthetics of the author's phrasing or his importance in terms of authority justify the use of direct quotation. Except in rare instances, quoted material is not transferred to the note cards; thus, direct quoting becomes less tempting during the subsequent writing phase when the student has recourse to his notes. Obviously the technique of making Xerox copies of stacks of articles and then writing with them directly at hand invites excessive quoting.

**Clarity and precision . . . speaking in system language.** The language we use in the commerce of our everyday lives is common language. We acquired our common language vocabulary and grammar by a process that was gradual, unsystematic, and mostly unconscious. Our everyday language serves us well, at least as long as the inevitable differences in word meanings assigned by different people do not produce serious failures of communication.

The language of science, specifically the language of research, is uncommon. The ongoing conversation of science, for which a research proposal is a plan of entry, is carried on in system languages in which each word must mean one thing to both writer and reader. Where small differences may matter a great deal, as in research, there must be a minimum of slippage between the referent object, the word used to stand for the object, and the images called forth by the word in the minds of listeners and readers.

The rules of invariate word usage give system languages a high order of precision. Minute or subtle distinctions can be made with relative ease. Evaluative language can be eliminated or clearly segregated from empirical descriptive language. More important, however, the language of research affords the reliability of communication that permits scientists to create a powerful interdependent research enterprise rather than limited independent investigations. When a chemist uses the system language of chemistry to communicate with another chemist, the word "element" has one and only one referent, is assigned to the referent on all occasions, is used for no other purpose within the language system, and consistently evokes the same image in the minds of everyone everywhere who has mastered the language.

Various domains of knowledge and various research enterprises are characterized by differing levels of language development. Some disciplines, such as anatomy or entomology, have highly developed and completely regularized language systems whereas others, particularly the behavioral sciences, employ languages still in the process of development. Irrespective of the area of investigation, however, the language of any research proposal must, as a minimum requirement, be systematic within itself. The words used in the proposal must have referents that are clear to the reader and must be used consistently to designate only one referent. When the investigation lies within a subject area with an existing language system, then, of course, the author is bound to the conventions of that system.

Obviously the student researcher should be familiar with the system languages that function in his area of proposed investigation. He must read and write both the specific language of the subject matter area and the more general languages common to his proposed methodology (statistics, experimental design, psychometrics, computer languages, etc.). Less obvious, however, is the fact that research proposals, by their exploratory nature, often demand the extension of existing language into new territory. Operations, observations, concepts, and relationships not previously specified within a language system must be assigned invariate word symbols by the investigator. More important, the reader must carefully be drawn into the agreement to make these same assignments.

Advisors misunderstand student proposals far more often than they disagree with what is proposed. The failure of communication often occurs precisely at the point where the proposal moves beyond the use of the existing system language. This problem involves a failure of careful invention rather than a failure of mastering technique or subject matter. The following rules may be of some help as the student attempts to translate his personal vision of the unknown into the form of a carefully specified public record.

1.  Never invent new words when existing system language is adequate. If the referent has a label that, in established use, excludes what you do not want and includes all that you do want, then it needs no new name.
2.  If there is reasonable doubt as to whether the word is in the system or the common domain, give the system definition as that obtaining for the proposal. The reader may give time and attention to the same question unless you put his mind at ease.

3. Words that have been assigned system meaning should not be used in their common language form. For example, the word "significant" should not be used to denote its common language meaning of "important" in a proposal involving the use of statistical analysis. The system language of inferential statistics assigns invariant meaning to the word "significant"; any other use invites confusion.

4. Where a system language word is to be used in either a more limited or a more expanded sense, make this clear when the word first is introduced in the proposal. If the norms for local style requirements permit, this is one of the legitimate uses of footnotes to the text.

5. Where it is necessary to assign invariant meaning to a common language word in order to communicate about something not already accommodated within the system language, the author should choose with great care. Words with strong evaluative overtones, words with a long history of ambiguity, and words that have well entrenched usage in common language, make poor candidates for elevation to system status. No matter how carefully the author operationalizes the new definition, it is always difficult for the reader to make new responses to familiar stimuli.

6. A specific definition is the best way to assign invariate meaning to a word. When only one or two words require such treatment, this can be accomplished in the text. Larger numbers may be set aside in a section of the proposal devoted to definitions. The best definition is one that describes the operations that are required to produce or observe the event or object. For example:

    a. A common language word is assigned invariate use — *Exclusion* will be deemed to have occurred when all four of the following situations obtain: The athlete no longer is issued playing equipment. The athlete is not allowed to engage in practice with the team. The athlete's name is stricken from the list of eligible players. The athlete is not allowed to attend regular team meetings.

    b. A system language word is employed with limitations not ordinarily assigned — *Closed Skill Sport* will be limited to those for which the current NCAA handbook provides a scoring system making the form of skill execution the sole or partial source of the point total used to determine a winner of the contest.

    c. System language word is operationalized by describing criterion — *Increased Motivation* will be presumed when, subsequent to any treatment condition, work output rises more than ten percent of the previous maximum.

    d. Common language word is operationalized by describing criterion

- *Injured Players* are defined as all participants withdrawn from the eligible player list by written notice of the team physician.

e. System language word is operationalized by describing procedure
   - *Reinforcement* will refer to the procedure of flashing the word "good" on the screen for one second following each successful trial.

f. Common language word is operationalized by describing procedure — *Instruction* will consist of ten five-minute sessions in which the teacher may employ any method of tuition so long as it (1) is in the water, (2) involves no assistive devices, and (3) includes no fewer than five attempts to locomote in the horizontal position.

**Editing . . . the care and nurture of a document.** A proposal is a working document. As a primary vehicle for communication with advisors, as a plan for action, and as a contract with the university, the student's proposal performs functions that are immediate and practical, not symbolic or aesthetic. Precisely because of these important functions, the proposal, in all of its public appearances at least, should be free from distracting mechanical errors and the irritating confusion of shoddy format.

At the privacy of his own desk, the student may use crossouts, scissors, paste, and rough drafts as part of the intellectual process through which a proposal evolves toward final form. When, however, the proposal is given to an advisor or presented to a seminar, the occasion is public and calls for an edited, formally prepared document. Every sentence must be examined and re-examined in terms of its clarity, grammar, and relationship with surrounding sentences. A mark of the neophyte writer is the tendency to resist changing a sentence once it is written, and even more so when it is typed. A sentence may be grammatically correct and still be awkward within its surroundings. If, in reading the sentence, a colleague, reviewer, or friend stumbles, or has to reread a sentence to understand its content, the sentence needs to be rewritten.

Aside from meticulous care in writing and rewriting, the most helpful procedure in undertaking editorial revision is to obtain the assistance of colleagues in reading the proposal for mechanical errors, lack of clarity, and inadequacies of content. An author can read the same error over and over without recognizing it — and the probability of discovery declines with each review. The same error may leap at once to the attention of even the most casual external reader. One useful trick that may improve the author's ability to spot mechanical errors is to read the sentences in reverse order, thus destroying the strong perceptual set created by the normal sequence of ideas.

Although format will be a matter of individual taste, or departmental regulation, several general rules may be used in designing the layout of the document:

1.  Use double spacing, substantial margins, and ample separation for major subsections. Crowding makes reading both difficult and unpleasant.
2.  Make ample use of graphic illustration. A chart or simple diagram can improve clarity and ease the difficult task of critical appraisal and advisement.
3.  Make careful and systematic use of headings. The system of headings recommended in the *Publication Manual of the American Psychological Association* (1974) is particularly useful for the design of proposals.
4.  Place in an appendix everything that is not immediately essential to the main tasks of the proposal. Allowing the reader to decide whether he will read supplementary material is both courtesy and good strategy.

**In search of a title . . . first impressions and the route to retrieval.** The title of the proposal is the first contact a reader has with the proposed research. First impressions, be they about people, music, food, or potential thesis topics, generate powerful anticipatory concepts of what is to follow. Shocking the reader by implying one content domain in the title and following with a different one in the body of the proposal is certain to evoke a strong negative response. Thus, the first rule in composing a title is to achieve reasonable parity between the images evoked by the title and the opening pages of the proposal.

The proposal title may well become the thesis title and therefore calls for careful consideration of all the functions it must serve and the standards by which it will be judged. The first function of the title is to identify content for the purpose of retrieval. Theses and dissertations have become a part of the public domain of the scholar. The increasing incidence of microcarding and microfilming has made the circulation of unpublished documents many times faster and far broader in geographic scope. Titling research has become, thereby, an important factor in sharing research.

In less sophisticated times, thesis titles could be carelessly constructed and the documents still discovered by diligent researchers who could take the time to investigate items that appeared no more than remotely related to their interests. Today, scholars stagger under the burden of sifting through enormous and constantly increasing quantities of material apparently pertinent to their domain. There is no recourse other than to be increasingly selective in documents actually retrieved and inspected. Hence, each title the researcher scans must present at least a moderate probability of being pertinent — on the basis of the title alone — or it will not be included on the reading list for review. In short, the degree to which the title communicates a concise, thorough, and unambiguous picture of the contents is the first factor governing whether a given report will enter the ongoing dialogue of the academic community.

Word selection should be governed more by universality of usage than by personal aesthetic judgment or peculiarly local considerations. Computer retrieval systems, such as MEDLAR, DATRIX, and ERIC, upon which more and more scholars are depending for leads to related studies in their research field, classify titles according to a limited set of key words. The researcher requests all studies categorized by the key words he thinks will best serve to retrieve studies of interest to him. Thus, both readers and writers of research reports must describe the research in similar terms or, in too many instances, they will not reach each other.

The title should describe as accurately as possible the exact nature of the main elements in the study. Although such accuracy demands the use of specific language, the title should be free of obscure technical terms or jargon that will be recognized only by small groups of researchers who happen to pursue similar questions within a narrow band of the knowledge domain.

*Components appropriate for inclusion in the title.* The elements most commonly considered for inclusion in the title are the dependent and independent variables, the performance component represented by the criterion task or tasks, the treatment or treatments to be administered, the model underlying the study, the purpose of the study (predicting, establishing relationships, or determining differences), and any particularly unusual contribution of the study.

Dependent and independent variables ordinarily should be included, although they may be presented under a more general rubric. For instance, the dependent variables of a study might be simple reaction time, discriminatory reaction time, movement time, and reflex time. In the title the four measures might appear as "neuromuscular responses." The performance components of the study also may be summarized into a single categorical term.

A clever author can, by careful selection of words, provide information in the title that a theory is being tested by using a word that often is associated with the theory. For instance, the title, "Generality of Single Motor Units in Postural and Manipulatory Muscles," implies that the investigator is testing the applicability of Henry's (1959) memory drum theory explaining the specificity of gross movements, to single motor units. Much has been communicated by including the single word "generality" in the title.

The ultimate purpose of the study in terms of predicting, establishing relationships, or determining differences can be expressed without providing an explicit statement. For example, when variables are expressed in a series — "Anthropometrics, Swimming Speed, and Shoulder-girdle Strength" — relationship generally is implied. If the same study were titled "Anthropometrics and Shoulder-girdle Strength of Fast and Slow Swimmers," the reader would anticipate a study in which differences were to be determined.

Any aspect of the study that is particularly unusual in terms of methodology, or that represents a unique contribution to the literature, should be included in the title. A treatment that is unusually long or of great magnitude, a method of observation that is creative or unusually accurate, and a particular site of measurement that sets the study apart from others, are examples of such aspects.

*Components inappropriate for inclusion in the title.* Such factors as population, research design, and instrumentation should not be included in the title unless they represent a substantial departure from similar studies. The population, for instance, should not be noted unless it is a population never sampled before, or is in some way an unusual target group. In the title, "Anthropometrics of World-Class High Jumpers," the population of subjects is critical to the rationale for the study. The population in "Running Speed, Leg Strength, and High Jumping of High School Boys," is not important enough to occupy space in the title.

Similarly, research design and instrumentation are not appropriate for inclusion in the title unless they represent an unusual approach to measurement or analysis. The type of research method expressed in "Physiologic Analysis of Pre-competitive Stress," is common in studies dealing with stress, and surely some other aspect of the study would make a more informative contribution to the title. The approach in "Phenomenological Analysis of Pre-competitive Stress," however, represents a unique approach and signals the reader that within the pages of the report he might expect to find information of an unusual kind.

*Mechanics of titling.* Mechanically, the title should be concise and should provide comfortable reading, free from elaborate or jarring constructions. Excessive length should be avoided because it dilutes the impact of the key elements presented; two lines generally should be adequate. Some retrieval systems place a word limitation on titles, thus enforcing brevity. Redundancies such as "Aspects of . . . ," "Comments on . . . ," "Study of . . . ," "Investigation of . . . ," "Inquiry into . . . ," and "An Analysis of . . . " are expendable. It is obvious that a careful investigation of a topic will include "aspects of" the topic, whereas the research report has as its entire purpose the communication of "comments on" the findings of a study. It is pointless to state the obvious in a title.

Attempts to include all subtopics of a study in the title sometimes result in elephantine rubrics. The decision to include or exclude mention of a subtopic should be made less in terms of an abstraction, such as "complete coverage," and more in terms of whether inclusion actually will facilitate appropriate retrieval.

One useful way to construct a title is to list all the elements that seem appropriate for inclusion, and then to weave them into various permutations until a title appears that satisfies both technical and aesthetic standards.

## SECTION 3. CONTENT OF THE PROPOSAL: IMPORTANT CONSIDERATIONS

**Spadework . . . the proper use of pilot studies.** The pilot study is an especially useful form of anticipation, and one too much neglected in student proposals. When it comes to convincing the skeptical reader (often your own advisor), no argument can be so effective as to write, "I tried it and here is how it worked."

It is difficult to imagine any proposal that could not be improved by the reporting of actual preliminary work. Whether it is to demonstrate the reliability of instrumentation, the practicality of procedures, the availability of volunteers, the variability of observed events as a basis for power tests, the capabilities of subjects, or the skill of the investigator, the modest pilot study is the best possible basis for making wise decisions in designing research.

The pilot study, for example, is an excellent means by which the sample size necessary to discover significant differences among experimental treatments may be determined.* From the findings of the pilot study, the experimenter may estimate expected means differences as well as the error variance per experimental unit. A thorough discussion and presentation of formulas for this technique are presented in Winer (1971).

The use of even a few subjects in an informal trial can reveal a fatal flaw before it can destroy months of work. The same trial may even provide a fortunate opportunity to improve the precision of the investigation or to streamline cumbersome methods. For all these reasons, students and advisors should not insist on holding stringent, formal standards for exploratory studies. A pilot study is a *pilot* study; its target is the practicality of proposed operations, not the creation of empirical truth.

The presentation of results from pilot studies sometimes does create a troublesome problem. The general rule is to make no more of the pilot study than it honestly is worth — most are no more than a report of experience

---

*Statistical significance, of course, is not synonymous with scientific significance in terms of the evolution of knowledge, or practical significance in terms of solving professional problems. Statistical significance largely depends on sample size and selection of the alpha level. It can be demonstrated between almost any two groups using almost any variable selected, if the sample size is large enough and the power of the test sufficiently high. Such differences between groups may be statistically significant but scientifically trivial and professionally worthless. The pilot study is an excellent device by which the probability of a Type I error may be estimated and an appropriate sample size selected. In this way the investigator can increase the probability that a statistically significant result will also reflect a difference of potential scientific and practical significance.

under less than perfectly controlled conditions – and to do so when the report will best illuminate the choices made in the proposal.

Brief reference to pilot work may be made in supporting the broad research strategies selected consequent to the review of research. Some pilot studies may, in fact, be treated as one of the works worthy of review. More commonly, however, the results of exploratory studies are used in supporting specific procedures proposed in the section dealing with methodology.

When the pilot study represents a formal and relatively complete research effort, it is proper to cite the work in some detail, including actual data. When the preliminary work has been informal or limited, it may be introduced as a footnote to the main text. In the latter case, it may be desirable to provide a more detailed account of the work in a section of the appendix, leaving the reader the choice of pursuing the matter further, if he wishes.

**Murphy's Law . . . anticipating the unexpected.** Murphy's Law dictates that, in the conduct of research, if there is anything that can go wrong, it probably will. This is accepted by experienced researchers and research advisors but rarely considered by the novice.

Within reasonable limits, the proposal is the place to provide for confrontation with the inexorable operation of Murphy's Law. Subject attrition cannot be prevented, but its effects can be circumscribed by careful planning. The potentially biasing effects created by non-returns in questionnaire studies can be examined and, to some degree, mitigated by plans laid carefully in the proposal. The handling of subjects in the event of equipment failure is far better considered at leisure, in writing the proposal, than in the face of an unanticipated emergency. Field research in the public schools can provide a range of surprises, including indisposed teachers, fire drills, and inclement weather, all better managed by anticipation than by snap decisions forged in the heat of sudden necessity.

Equipment failure may interrupt carefully timed data collection sequences, or temporary computer breakdowns may delay data processing and analysis. At best these contingencies may place constraints on the time schedule of the study, and at worst may demand substitutions or substantive changes in the procedures. Each step of the experimental process should be studied with regard to potential difficulty, and plans in the event of a problem should be stated in the appropriate place within the proposal. For instance, if unequal subject attrition occurs across groups, the type of analysis to be used with unequal $N$'s should be stated in the analysis section of the proposal.

It is impossible to anticipate everything that can happen. A good proposal, however, provides contingency plans for the most important problems that may arise in the course of conducting the study.

**Anticipating the analysis ... do it now.** The proposal is the proper place to reveal the exact nature of the analysis, as well as anticipated plans in the event of emergency. For many students, especially master's candidates, the analysis — if statistical — may represent new knowledge, recently acquired and not fully digested. In addition, the customary time limitation of 12 to 16 months by which the master's candidate finds himself bound adds to the difficulty. The candidate may even be in the middle of his first formal course in techniques of data reduction and analysis during the same period of time he is constructing his proposal. Consequently, students find themselves in the awkward position of having to write lucidly about the nature of their analytic tools without yet knowing the entire armamentarium available. As untenable as this position is, and as much sympathy as may be generated by the student's advisor or friends, the omission of a full consideration of the analysis in the proposal may prove to be fatal. Countless unfortunates have found themselves in possession of shoe boxes heaped with unanalyzable data — all because the analysis was supposed to "take care of itself." A step-by-step anticipation of the analysis to be used also is a double check on the experimental design.

Descriptive, survey, and normative studies require extensive data reduction to produce meaningful quantitative descriptions and summaries of the phenomena of interest. Techniques of determining sample characteristics may be different from those anticipated on the basis of pilot results; or, the study sample may be skewed, resulting in the need to discuss techniques for normalizing the data.

Statistical techniques are founded on assumptions relating to sample characteristics and on assumptions pertaining to the relationship between the sample and its respective population. The methods the student intends to use to determine whether the sample meets the assumptions explicit within his anticipated analysis should be clearly stated. For example, many statistical techniques must be used only when one or more of the following assumptions are met: (a) normal distribution of the sample; (b) random and independent selection of scores; (c) linear relationships of variables; (d) homogeneity of variance among groups (in regression analysis, this is called homoscedasticity); (e) independence of sample means and variances; and (f) units of measure of the dependent variable on a ratio scale.

How will the student determine which assumptions have been met? What analyses will be used in the event that the assumptions are not met? Will the planned analyses be appropriate in the event subjects are lost and unequal cell frequencies result?

The analysis segment of the proposal should be outlined to correspond to the objectives of the study, so that each analysis will yield evidence relating to a corresponding hypothesis. In addition, the reader should be able to determine how all data collected are to be analyzed. If data are to be presented in tabular or graphic form, an example of one such table, including predicted figures, often will be helpful to the reader. The purpose of a table or figure in a research report is to summarize material and to supplement the text in making it clearly understandable. Tables and graphic presentation may serve the same purpose in a proposal.

Because of their display quality, the inclusion of tables in the proposal may expose errors of research design. For instance, some committee readers may not detect the use of an incorrect error term from a reading of the text, but one glance at the degrees of freedom column in an analysis of variance table may reveal the error. If several tables are listed and proposed, analysis of variance comparisons of non-independent variables may be exposed.

If the analysis activity of the project is studied carefully in advance, many headaches – as well as heartaches – may be avoided. It may seem to take an inordinate amount of time to plan the analysis, but it is time that will not have to be spent again. As the analyses are completed, the results can immediately be inserted in the prepared tables, and the researcher can complete his project with a feeling of fulfillment rather than a frantic scramble to make sense out of a puzzle for which some of the pieces may prove to be missing.

**The statistical well . . . drinking the greatest draught.** Students can usually expect help from their advisors with the design of statistical analysis. At minimum, an experienced advisor will have some suggestions about the type of analysis that would be most appropriate for the proposed investigation. Many departments of physical education include measurement and evaluation specialists who have statistical consultation with graduate students as a primary part of their professorial responsibility. Other departments work closely with outside statistical consultants who may be housed in departments of educational psychology, psychology, computer science, or business.

The student should not, however, operate under the faulty impression that when the data are collected, they can be turned over to a handy statistical expert who, having an intimate relationship with the local computer, will magically return raw data in the finished form of findings and conclusions. Just as the student cannot expect the analysis of data to take care of itself, neither can the student expect a statistical consultant to take care of it.

The assistance of a statistician, invaluable though it may be, ordinarily is limited to the technology of design and data analysis. The conceptual demands of the study and the particular form and characteristics of the data generated are the investigator's province – to be explained to the consultant, not vice versa. Likewise, the interpretation of results is a logical, not a technical, operation and thus is a responsibility for which only the investigator is properly prepared.

To obtain technical help from an advisor, the student should be prepared to provide basic concepts about the content domain of the investigation, including a concise review of what is to be studied, and a preliminary estimate of alternative designs that might be appropriate to the demands of the proposed research. In addition, whether advice concerning design, statistics, or computer programing is sought from the student's project advisor, from a departmental specialist, or from an expert source external to the department, there are basic communication factors that must be considered if the student is to glean the most information and help for the smallest cost in valuable consultation time.

*Rule 1: Understand the consultant's frame of reference.* As with any other situation involving extended communication, it is useful to know enough about the language, predilections, and knowledge base of the consultant to avoid serious misunderstandings and ease the process of initiating the transaction. The consultant ordinarily is a professional whose primary interest is in the process of research design and statistical analysis. He uses a system language unique to statistics, and appreciates those who understand at least the rudiments of his vocabulary. Correspondingly, he will not necessarily understand the system language to be used in the proposal, nor will he know peculiar characteristics of the data. For example, it cannot be assumed that he knows that strength fatigue curve data comprise replicated measures. Similarly, it would be unlikely for him to know whether data of this kind are normally distributed across trials.

The consultant cannot be expected to make decisions that relate to the purpose of the study, such as those regarding the balance between internal and external validity. Some designs may maximize the validity of the differences that may be found, but correspondingly trade off external validity, and thus the generalizability of the findings. Decisions concerning the acceptability of such research designs must be made by the proposer of the study. The grounds for such a determination rest in the purpose of the study and thus in conceptual work completed long before the consultation interview.

The consultant can be expected to evaluate a proposed experimental design, assist in selection from a group of alternative designs, or suggest more efficient designs that have not been considered. He often can be most helpful, however, if preliminary models for design and statistical analysis have been proposed. This provides a starting place for discussion and often can serve as a vehicle for considering characteristics of the data that will impose special demands.

Finally, the consultant can provide information about computer programs available, the appropriateness of a particular program for the proposed design, and the entry techniques into these programs. Again, some preliminary preparation by the student (talking with other students presently engaged in computer use, reviewing material on computer language and programs, and visiting the computer center to update himself on available services) can make the consultant's advisory task easier and work to guarantee an optimal selection of procedures for processing raw data.

Normally, the statistics specialist in a university setting is besieged by frantic graduate students and busy faculty colleagues, all in addition to the demands of his own students. Further, he may be responsible for the management of one or more functions in his own administrative unit or in the computer center. Finally, as an active scientist he is attempting to conduct his own research. Both the picture and the lesson should be equally clear to the student seeking assistance. Statisticians are busy people. They can provide effective assistance only when investigators come with accurate expectations for the kind of help a consultant can properly provide, and come fully prepared to exercise their own responsibilities in the process.

*Rule 2: Learn the language.* The system languages of measurement, computer science, experimental design, and both inferential and descriptive statistics are used in varying degrees in the process of technical consultation for many research proposals. No one, least of all an experienced consultant, expects fluent mastery in the novice. The student must, however, have a working knowledge of fundamental concepts. These ordinarily include measures of central tendency and variability, distribution models, and the concept of statistical significance. Basic research designs, such as those described in introductory research method books, should be familiar to any novice.

It is, of course, preferable to complete at least one statistics course before attempting any study that will demand the analysis of quantitative data. If, as sometimes is the case, the student is learning basic statistics concurrent with the preparation of the proposal, special effort will have to be concentrated on preparing for consultations concerning design and analysis. The situation will be awkward at best, although many advisors will remain sympathetic and patient if the student is honest about his limitations and willing to exert himself heroically once it becomes clear which tools and concepts must be mastered.

Beyond the problem of mastering enough of the language to participate in a useful discussion is the more subtle problem of understanding the particular analysis selected for the study. The student must not allow himself to drift into the position of using a statistical tool he really does not understand — even one endorsed and urged upon him by the most competent of advisors. Ultimately, the student will have to make sense out of the results obtained through any analysis. At that point, shallow or incorrect interpretations will quickly betray a failure to understand the nature of the analysis. Expert technical advice can be an invaluable asset in devising a strong proposal, but in the final analysis, such advice cannot substitute for the competence of the investigator.

*Rule 3: Understand the proposed study.* If the novice researcher lacks sufficient understanding of his own study to identify and ask important and explicit questions, that lack is a major obstacle to a successful consultation. Only when the consultant understands the questions of central interest in the study can he begin to translate them into the steps of statistical analysis. Further, a host of specific constraints associated with the nature of the study will condition the advisor's decision about which analysis to recommend.

The student should be ready to provide answers to each of the following questions:

1.  What are the independent variables of the study?
2.  What are the dependent variables of the study?
3.  What are the organismic variables of the study?
4.  What is the measurement scale of each variable (nominal, ordinal, interval, or ratio)?
5.  What are the reliability and validity of the instruments used to produce the scores for each variable?
6.  What are the population distribution characteristics for each of the variables?
7.  What difference value between dependent variables would be of *practical* significance?
8.  What are the monetary, safety, ethical, or educational risks involved if a Type I error is made?
9.  What is the nature of the loss if a Type II error is made?

In summary, before he consults with a technical specialist the student must be able to express exactly what he wants the study to be designed to accomplish, identify the help he needs in producing such a design, and provide all the explicit details the consultant will need in formulating his advice.

**Informed consent . . . the protection of human subjects.** Many universities employ a system of mandatory review for all research proposals involving the use of human subjects. The purpose of such review usually is to protect the health and welfare of the subjects or to ensure ethical procedures on the part of the investigator.

In recent years the definition of subject health and welfare has expanded, as a greater volume of diverse research activity has necessitated a broader definition of what constitutes ethical behavior for the investigator and reasonable protection for the subject. The point we wish to emphasize here is at once broader and more basic than the traditional concern for the safety of the subject; every human has a right not to be used by other people, research workers especially included.

The right not to be used applies with equal force to fifth graders, college sophomores, and members of professional athletic teams. Subjects who cooperate in scientific investigations have a right to know what they are getting into and a right to give or withhold their cooperation on the basis of that information. The fact that one uses volunteers, or even paid subjects, does not alter their human right not to be treated as chattels. That this rule has so often been ignored in the past accounts in large measure for the difficulties, both obvious and subtle, in obtaining cooperation from prospective subjects.

There has been divided opinion among social scientists on the degree to which use of psychometric instruments and questionnaires should be circumscribed by the use of procedures to protect the basic rights of subjects. This is an issue to be discussed with advisors during the preparation of the proposal. Our own position on this matter is unequivocal. Concern for the rights of subjects should attend the use of all paper and pencil instruments. The procedures employed in taking reasonable account of the subject's right to be informed may be much less elaborate than those used in an experiment involving physical discomfort or some degree of risk, but they should be designed with care and applied with scrupulous uniformity.

It is the ubiquitousness of questionnaires and the seeming innocuousness of psychometric instruments that present a special danger, a danger made more lethal because it is so much less obvious than the hazards involved in medical, pharmaceutical, or psychiatric research. To employ paper and pencil instruments without regard for the rights of subjects produces several unfortunate results. Each time people are involved in a situation in which it is assumed that they have no right to the privacy of their inner thoughts, one more small instruction has been given that such is the case. In contrast, when the investigator treats entry into the inner thoughts of a subject as a special privilege, granted by a consenting human as an act of informed cooperation, the opposite instruction is given and powerfully reinforced.

Of equal importance for the evolution of knowledge, improper use of paper and pencil tests has become an insidious pollution that already has eroded the effectiveness of these valuable instruments. Form questionnaires, pushed under the noses of subjects without explanation, cannot be taken as serious matters of consequence when they are filled out. When the instrument is not made to seem important, when the subject is not treated as though he or she were important, and when this takes place repeatedly over a lifetime, a kind of "case hardening" occurs, which leads to careless, ill-considered responses, and even to deliberately falsified answers. Such data can only produce meaningless and disruptive results. Subject populations are a vital resource for the investigator and, like any fragile resource, must be used in ways that preserve them for the future.

As a minimum, the student should consider including the following procedures in any proposal involving human subjects:

1.  Each subject is to be informed of the general nature of the investigation and, within reasonable limits, of his own role. A written script may be used in transmitting such information and should be included in an appendix to the proposal.
2.  Each subject is to have the opportunity, after reasonable consideration, to sign a document affirming that he has been informed of the general nature of the investigation and that he has consented to give

his full cooperation. A copy of this form should be included in the appendix to the proposal (see the specimen form for "informed consent" in Appendix C).

3.  Each subject should receive an explanation of all treatment procedures to be used.
4.  Each subject should receive an explanation of any discomforts or risks involved.
5.  Each subject should receive an offer to answer any questions concerning purposes, procedures, discomforts, or risks.
6.  Each subject should be instructed that he is free to withdraw consent and discontinue participation in the study at any time.
7.  Each subject should be offered an opportunity to receive feedback on the results of the investigation at an appropriate later date.

Arguments to the effect that such procedures introduce unknown experimental bias effects are, in most cases, spurious. All contacts between investigators and subjects hold the potential for generating unknown effects, these procedures no more than any other. On the other hand, these procedures, quite aside from their ethical import, can exercise a measure of control over one of the most capricious of all variables — subject cooperation.

If it seems essential to withhold some specific item of information from subjects, then, after careful consideration of alternative courses of action, certainly it must be withheld. In almost all cases, however, there will be some important information that can be given to the subject as a basis for his decision to accept or decline participation. The proposal must present an explicit method for dealing with subjects that clearly indicates the nature of any omission. Further, the proposal must indicate procedures for promptly and thoroughly debriefing subjects whenever information has been withheld.

The basic rule is to treat subjects the way you would like to be treated as far as the specific exigencies of the study will permit. Any decision to do otherwise demands both compelling rationale and the most careful scrutiny.

**The scientific state of mind . . . proof, truth, and rationalized choices.** Scientific inquiry is not so much a matter of elaborate technology or even rigorous method as it is a particular state of mind. The processes of science rest, in the end, upon how scientists regard the world and their work. Although some aspects of scientific thinking are subtle and elusive, others are not. These latter, the basic attitudinal prerequisites for the conduct of scientific inquiry, are reflected in the way a novice speaks and writes about his proposed research. More directly, his proposal will reflect the degree to which he has internalized critical attitudes toward such matters as proof, truth, and publicly rationalized choices.

What matters is not the observance of particular conventions concerning phrasing, but fundamental ways of thinking that are reflected in the selection of words. When, for example, a student writes, "The purpose of this study is to prove (or, to demonstrate) that . . . ," there always is the dangerous possibility that he means to do just that — to prove what he has decided must be true.

Such phrasing cannot be dismissed simply as awkward or naive. A student capable of writing such a sentence without hearing at once its dangerous implications is a student with a fundamental defect in his preparation. He should be allowed to go no further until he has understood both the nature of proof and the purpose of research in the scientific enterprise, for clearly he understands neither.

Proof, if it exists at all in any useful sense, is a probabilistic judgment based upon an accumulation of observations. Ordinarily, only a series of careful replications can lead to the level of confidence implied by the word "proved." Research is not an attempt to prove or demonstrate, it is an attempt to ask a careful question and to allow the nature of things to dictate the answer. The difference between "attempting to prove" and "seeking proof" is subtle but critical, and a scientist must never confuse the two.

If scientists have no illusions about proof, it is wrong, nonetheless, to believe that they never care about the direction of results obtained from their research. As humans, they often are painfully aware of the distinction between results that will be fortunate or unfortunate for their developing line of thought. As scientists, however, they recognize the irrelevance (and even the danger) of allowing personal feelings to intrude in the business of seeking knowledge. In the end, the researcher must sit down before his facts like a child, and allow himself to be instructed. His task lies in arranging the context for instruction, so that the answers to his questions will be clear, but the content of the lesson lies in the nature of the world.

A second critical sign of the student's ability to adopt the scientific viewpoint is the general way the matter of truth is treated in his proposal. When a student writes, "The purpose of this study is to discover the actual cause of . . . ," there is the danger that he thinks it possible to do just that — to discern the ultimate face of reality at a single glance. The most fundamental remediation will be required if he ever is to understand, much less conduct, scientific inquiry.

The experienced researcher seeks and reveres veridical knowledge; he may even choose to think of research as the search for truth, but he understands the elusive, fragile, and probabilistic nature of scientific truth. Knowledge is regarded as a tentative decision about the world, always held contingent upon the content of the future.

The business of the researcher is striving to understand. Correspondingly, he places a high value on hard-won knowledge. He holds his truths gently, however, and speaks and writes accordingly. It is not necessary to lard a proposal with reservations, provisos, and disclaimers such as, "it seems." It is necessary to write with respect for the complexity of things and with modesty for what can be accomplished. The researcher's highest expectation for any study is a small but perceptible shift in the scale of evidence. He deals not in the heady stuff of truth, "establishing actual causes," but in hard-won increments of probability.

A third sign by which to estimate the student's scientific maturity is his ability (and willingness) to examine alternative interpretations of evidence, plausible rival hypotheses, facts that bid to discomfort his theoretical framework, and considerations that reveal the limitations of his methodology. It is important not only to lay out the alternatives for the reader but to explain the grounds for choice among them. The student who neither acknowledges alternatives nor rationalizes his choices simply does not understand research well enough to bother with a proposal.

The mature researcher feels no compulsion to provide perfect interpretations or to make unassailably correct choices. He does the best he can within the limits of existing knowledge and his present situation. He does feel compelled, however, to make clearly rationalized choices from among carefully defined alternatives; this is one reason readers outside the scientific community find research reports tedious in their attention to detail and explanation. It is the public quality of the researcher's reasoning that makes a community of scientific enterprise possible, not the construction of a facade of uniform certainty and perfection.

Student-conducted research often contains choices that must be rationalized less by the shape of existing knowledge and the dictates of logic and more by the homely facts of logistics — time, costs, skills achieved, and available facilities. The habit of public clarity in describing and rationalizing choices must begin there — with the way things are. An honest accounting of hard and often imperfect choices is a firm step for the student toward achieving the habits of a good researcher — the scientific state of mind.

# References

American Psychological Association. *Publication manual of the American Psychological Association.* Washington, D.C.: American Psychological Association, 1974.

Bauernfeind, R. H. Research notes. *Phi Delta Kappan,* 1968, *50,* 126-128.

Campbell, W. C. *Form and style in thesis writing.* Boston: Houghton Mifflin, 1969.

Davitz, J.R., & Davitz, L.J. *A guide for evaluating research plans in psychology and education.* New York: Teachers College Press, 1967.

Henry, F.M. Increased response latency for complicated movements and a "memory drum" theory of neuromotor reaction. *Research Quarterly,* 1960, *31,* 448-457.

Krathwohl, D.R. *How to prepare a research proposal.* Syracuse: Syracuse University Bookstore, 1966.

Kroll, W.P., & Peterson, K.H. Cross validation of the Booth Scale. *Research Quarterly,* 1966, *37,* 66-70.

Pelton, B. A need for replication in research in health, physical education and recreation. *Research Quarterly,* 1970, *41,* 613-615.

Winer, B.J. *Statistical principles in experimental design,* 2nd edition. New York: McGraw-Hill, 1971.

# PART III

## Specimen Proposals

The three specimen proposals reviewed here were selected with several intentions. First, the authors wished to display proposals at very different stages of development — near completion, intermediate, and preliminary. Second, they sought to display proposals within distinctly different research traditions — laboratory/experimental, field-based evaluational, and historical. Third, it seemed important to display real proposals with all their naturally occurring limitations and problems.

None of the three proposals presented here was rewritten beyond a few editorial changes. The specimen proposals are working documents that represented part of the learning process for three real graduate students. The faculty advisors in the student's respective institutions had provided either no guidance at all in the preparation of the proposal as in the case of the proposal at the earliest stage of development, or were somewhere in the midst of the complicated process of review, consultation, and revision. As a consequence, these documents in no way represent the final product that would be typical of the institutions concerned, or the final product that was actually produced by the three students. The third proposal, in a preliminary stage, and the second, in the intermediate stage, are plans for master's theses. The first proposal, somewhat nearer to completion, was a draft for a doctoral dissertation. Other specimens of doctoral level proposals may be seen in items 15 and 16 listed in Appendix B.

# PROPOSAL NUMBER 1
# INTRODUCTORY NOTE

This specimen proposal is a plan that became the basis for a doctoral dissertation. A small number of elements in the proposal were subject to minor modification to increase the utility of the document for this review. The document reproduced here is the third draft of a proposal for a classical experimental laboratory study. It will be obvious to the reader that considerable thought, study, and even preliminary data collection already have been invested. The problems represented in this proposal may be characterized primarily as inadequate communication between author and reader, difficulties with content organization, and breakdowns in the relationships between proposal components. With this draft the investigator was relatively far along the "Twenty Steps to a Proposal" path (approximately Step 18) and enough information is included for the reader to have a clear picture of the questions the researcher plans to ask. Happily, this proposal has reached the stage where, with the completion of the suggested changes, it can serve as a thorough and well-planned basis for the writing of a dissertation. The literature section must be completed, but when the data are collected and analyzed, the results can simply be inserted into the proposal format. The single remaining task is to interpret the results within the frame of reference established by the rationale and supporting evidence. The long hours of toil the student has invested in the patient planning, writing, and editing of this proposal will be paid with interest in the final rewards of excitement and fulfillment that accompany the culmination of a meticulously conducted research study.

**1**     The title is functional if not elegant. It portrays with accuracy and economy the main elements in the proposed study: the topic of central interest (the dependent variable), independent variables, and subject population. By the simple strategy of using the construction "under conditions (a) and (b) in populations (x) and (y)," a great deal is communicated about the nature of the study and the contrasts to be undertaken in the analysis. Given the title, a reader with no more than a modest background in the area can make useful inferences about the investigator's interest in the variable of pain tolerance.

    As you read the proposal it will be useful to note some of the elements the author has elected not to include in the title. Given the standards for titling established in this monograph, would you have made different decisions, leading to a more inclusive title?

PAIN TOLERANCE UNDER DISTRACTED AND

NON-DISTRACTED CONDITIONS IN FEMALE

ATHLETES AND NONATHLETES

**1**

A Thesis Proposal

Presented to

The Supervising Committee

University of Erehwon

In Partial Fulfillment

of the Requirements for the Degree

Doctor of Philosophy

by

A Graduate Student

March 1969

**2**     This is a sound opening paragraph. It immediately establishes the close association of the topic of pain with physical activity and the professions concerned with athletic performance. The phrase ". . . thus it is of special interest to physical educators" introduces a non sequitur, however, that will bother some readers. There is no need to write with a heavy hand. Particularly in the crucial opening paragraph, an accurate and simple presentation of the facts is all that is required.

**3**     In addition to explaining a central variable in the proposed study, the second paragraph will serve to interest many readers by placing the subject matter within the realm of nearly universal human experience. The closing sentence provides a clear lead into the proposed investigation.

## INTRODUCTION

Pain frequently is a companion to strenuous **2** physical activity and is thought to be a limiting factor in physical endurance. It has been postulated that capacity to tolerate pain is a contributor to athletic success; thus it is of special interest to physical educators.

Although most individuals' pain thresholds-- **3** the point at which they just begin to perceive pain--are relatively similar, the range of tolerance to pain among individuals is great. Variations in individuals' willingness to tolerate pain apparently are due to the psychological component of the perception of stimuli. Just as persons may, from within their individualized life styles, perceive visual, auditory, or textural cues differently, so some may perceive a given level of pain as excessive while others may perceive the same level as tolerable. It might be antici-

**4**     The author probably intended this paragraph to explain and justify the use
of a pain tolerance test in the proposed study. For many readers, however,
the process of deciphering the relationship between the cryptic first sentence
and the preceding paragraph will obscure the crucial introduction of pain
tolerance as a measured variable. The complex structure of the final sentence
ensures that the overall effect will be disruptive rather than helpful. Most
readers will arrive at the discussion of athletes and nonathletes in the paragraph that follows, still thinking about Petrie and wondering what they
missed. Only a painstaking rewrite will make it possible to continue the line
of discussion established in the preceding paragraph, introduce the concept
of pain tolerance as a variable, and lead logically into the new line of discussion in the next paragraph.

pated that dedicated athletes would be extremely high in pain tolerance inasmuch as grueling training and physical pain are requisites to success in athletics. Whether athletes differ from nonathletes in pain threshold is not known.

One explanation for individual differences in pain tolerance is that of Petrie (28), who has hypothesized that individuals systematically modify stimuli so that all people can be categorized into one of three classes: reducers, who consistently perceive and report a stimulus to be less intense than its objective measurement; augmentors, who consistently perceive a stimulus to be greater than its objective measurement; and moderators, who neither augment nor reduce stimuli systematically.

A second explanation for psychological **4** differences in sensory perception is that the meaning, or apperception, of pain for an individual is related to his ability to tolerate

5    Previous studies have shown relationships between other types of distractors and pain tolerance; however, the author argues here that the motor component of performance itself may be so intensely consuming to the athlete that it serves as a powerful distraction. The careful reader might discern that the author has further suggested that this distraction effect could be more powerful in athletes than in nonathletes. Many readers, however, would miss one or both of these vital points. The logic would be much more clear if the paragraph began with a statement about distraction, which then led into the point concerning absorption in the athletic task.

it. Apperception, then, is proposed as either
singly, or in combination, a function of perceptual type, personality, childhood experiences, and motivation.

Evidence exists to support the hypothesis
that athletes differ from nonathletes in their
tolerance for painful stimuli, as well as in
their apperception of pain. In at least two
studies (31, 32) which included pain as one
sensory modality, male athletes were classified as sensory reducers. In addition, male
and female athletes consistently scored higher
on the personality trait of extroversion, a
factor which may influence an athlete's apperception of pain both in himself and in
others.

An equally feasible but unsupported explana- 5
tion for the high tolerance levels of athletes
is that they are more motivated by physical
challenges than nonathletes. An athlete may
become so intent upon displaying neuromuscular skill that he is distracted from his

**6**    It is *never* permissible to indicate that something was "reported" without making it available to the reader through an appropriate citation.

**7**    In a preceding paragraph, it has been noted that the subjects who were used to establish the relationship between pain tolerance and physical activity have been males. The investigator here seeks to add another dimension by employing female subjects. This important contribution is not made explicitly clear, however, and might easily be overlooked by the reader.

sensations of pain. Various types of cognitive tasks, used as distractors, have been
reported as significantly raising pain toler- **6**
ance levels.

Several questions regarding the relationships of pain tolerance and neuromuscular
performance remain unanswered. Whether fe- **7**
male athletes tolerate more pain than non-
athletic females is not known, nor is it
known whether athletes, when performing a
neuromuscular skill task under painful conditions, will be more able to tolerate pain
than nonathletes under the same painful conditions. Little is known about the extent
to which pain produces a deterioration of
neuromuscular skill, yet one would expect
that athletes, in psychologically reducing
pain sensations, might postpone or eliminate
skill deterioration substantially more than
nonathletes who may be concentrating on the
painfulness of the stimulus. Do female athletes apperceive pain differently from fe-

**8**    The use of the word "compare" to denote a situation in which differences are
the issue is a violation of proper word usage in statistics. The word "compare" generally is employed in reference to correlational techniques, and the
investigator clearly proposes to test for significant differences between group
means.

males who are nonathletes?  Do female athletes tolerate more pain under conditions of
distraction than do female nonathletes?  Formulating answers to these questions is the
purpose of this study.

## PURPOSE

The purpose of this study is to determine
whether female athletes differ from nonathletes on the variables of pain threshold,
pain tolerance, distracted pain tolerance,
and psychological apperception of pain.  A
second purpose is to compare the effect of     **8**
a neuromuscular distraction on pain tolerance of athletic and nonathletic females.
The final purpose of this study is to examine
the relationship among pain apperception,
pain threshold, pain tolerance, and distracted
pain tolerance.

**9**     The first definition suggests that "just noticeable pain" also requires a definition.
          The reader will notice minor variations in the wording and format used for
the seven definitions. This is a common problem for novice researchers and
demands close attention to exact detail of expression. Such syntactical shifts
can be surprisingly distracting for many readers.

**10**    This really is no definition at all. To be useful (and consistent), this definition should be written in terms of the subject's performance. Specifying
particular operations is the surest way of producing an unambiguous definition.

## DEFINITIONS

To facilitate reading the remainder of the proposal, terms are defined below that either are unique to the system language used in pain literature, or are operationalized for the proposed study.

1. Pain threshold is that amount of direct 9 current in milliamps that gives rise to just noticeable pain.

2. Pain tolerance is the greatest amount of direct current, up to 30 milliamps, that a subject will voluntarily withstand.

3. Distracted tolerance is the greatest amount of direct current, up to 30 milliamps, that a subject will voluntarily withstand while performing the neuromuscular skill test.

4. Neuromuscular distraction task is completion of an electric hole-type steadiness test. 10

**11**     In the opening sentence the author has provided a simple organizing framework for examining the related literature. Although the categories do not arise from any elegant conceptual theory, they do accomplish two useful functions: (1) they form a convenient basis for organizing the review, and (2) they provide the reader with a quick survey of the main targets for previous research and thereby a sense of the stream into which the present study must be inserted.

5. Psychological pain apperception is the score attained by a subject on a seventeen-item psychological test of pain apperception.

6. Athlete refers to the membership of an individual on a varsity basketball team, where membership involves competition for positions, regularly scheduled practices and interschool competition, and receipt of a scholarship.

7. Nonathlete refers to individuals who are not members of a varsity team in any sport, and who do not compete on an intramural or varsity level in an individual or dual sport.

## RELATED LITERATURE

The pertinent literature of pain may be classified under the categories of physiology of pain, threshold and tolerance parameters, factors related to pain tolerance, pain dis-

11

**12**     Although this vital point is related to all the research in the five categories, it seems to deserve the visibility of status as a separate paragraph. The point easily could be expanded to the profit of the reader.

**13**     The material in this paragraph is intended as a general introduction to all the following categories. The flow of ideas would run more smoothly if that function were made clear in the opening sentence (some readers might think that the review already was under way). A closing sentence or two should be added to form a bridge between the introductory remarks and the first category in the review that follows.

traction, pain as affected by handedness,

and pain responses of athletes and nonathletes.

Pain usually is defined introspectively by

the subject (18).   This limitation is one of      **12**

the problems in the scientific study of

pain (39).

Several theories of pain sensation have           **13**

been prominent through the years (7, 15).

When Aristotle named the so-called five senses,

pain was not one of them.   It was thought to

be an emotion, a quality of the soul.   This

was known as the "emotion" theory of pain.

The second general theory of pain was the

"intensive" theory, which was prominent in

the mid-nineteenth century.   It held that

pain was the result of intensive stimulation

of any sensory receptor.   Third was the "sen-

sory" theory which gained widespread support

in the late nineteenth century.   This theory

held that pain was a sensation with its own

distinct sensory mechanisms.

**14**     This section is not directly applicable to the proposed research. Most readers, unable to make this initial decision, will dutifully read on until they discover, with less than charitable feeling, that the author has been engaging in a largely ceremonial excursion. The section should be eliminated or summarized. Truly pertinent information could be included within the later discussion of Pain Threshold and Pain Tolerance.

**15**     The theory reported in reference (26) is introduced, but the discussion terminates abruptly with a new reference (20), which is not a primary source. Tossing in the additional reference can only serve here to confuse the reader. Further, unless there is some compelling reason, primary sources always are to be preferred. If the reader is interested in pursuing a point he will not wish to be directed to what one author writes about what another author wrote.

Physiology of Pain **14**

The cutaneous receptor for pain has usually been considered to be the free nerve endings which form a closely interlocking network of fine fibrils in the most superficial skin layers (15). Livingston (22), however, questions this concept, saying that the old idea that the bare nerve endings are exclusively responsible for pain cannot be validated in all situations. The evidence indicates that pain and touch must come from the concurrent activation of many different sensory fibers of various sizes and distributions. Several current authors object to the specialization theory of sensory nerve cells. Melzach and Wall (26) postulate that some receptors are **15** specialized, while others may respond to a wide range of stimuli with a characteristic firing pattern for each. In fact, if any stimulus is intense enough, specificity is overwhelmed and the dominant sensation is one

of pain (20). In an effort to present experimental conclusiveness of non-specificity,
Casey (4) sought to determine if in the awake
squirrel monkey there were thalamic neurons
that responded only to noxious stimuli. Using
microelectrodes in three thalamic regions
believed to be associated with pain sensation
and testing 323 units, he found none that
responded to pain alone. Rather, the pain
stimuli were associated with a greater shift
in the discharge frequency than were innocuous
stimuli.

Impulses initiated by pain are propagated
by two types of fibers. The larger are myeli-
nated A fibers, approximately eight microns
in diameter, that conduct impulses at a speed
of 25M/sec, while the smaller are unmyelinated
C fibers, about one micron in diameter, that
conduct impulses at a speed of 1M/sec. The
difference in speed is thought to account for
the two reported components of pain: a sudden,
sharp sensation, followed by a more prolonged

**16**     Again, primary rather than secondary sources are more appropriate in a
research proposal.

**17**     An attentive reader will immediately want to know the source for this important point about exercise. Although he might suppose that the student-
level textbooks cited in (20) and (13) contained some reference to appropriate original sources, he also may resent being subject to a paper chase.

aching sensation (20). The pain receptor is
thought to be stimulated by histamine (20)
and/or bradykinin (13), both of which are **16**
released when cells are damaged and both of
which are present as metabolic biproducts of
sustained and demanding mucular contractions
such as those occurring during exercise. **17**
There is some integration at the thalamic
level; however, the cortex is necessary for
accurate determination of intensity and
location.

## Pain Threshold and Tolerance

Threshold and tolerance are the usual variables recorded in the measurement of pain.
Unfortunately, their definition may vary from
author to author. Wolff (37) has noted that
lack of agreement in definition of variables
makes comparisons of studies difficult. He
suggests that pain threshold be defined as
that stimulus value which gives rise to just
noticeable pain as judged by the subjects.

**18**    This paragraph contains an unexpected shift of verb tense from the preceding paragraph. In a review of this kind, occasional shifts between present and past tense may go unnoticed by the reader. Change in tense actually may have some utility when it is used to underscore such subtle distinctions as the difference between events reported and the report itself. Here, however, the shifting voices of the two adjacent paragraphs seem discontinuous, even though the basic subject (Gelfand's report) remains the same. A good, simple rule is to write in the past tense, reserving shifts to the present for particular and limited purposes. The proposal should, of course, employ the passive voice wherever an action of the researcher is concerned. This standard holds irrespective of the tense involved; in proposals, unlike research reports, all three tenses find common use. Tradition demands that the person of the investigator be subdued by an impersonal tone.

There is little disagreement over the definition and measurement of pain threshold; however, two discrete methods of defining and measuring pain tolerance have been reported. In contrast to Wolff, who measured tolerance from onset of stimulus to the upper limit of pain an individual was willing to accept under experimental conditions, Gelfand (11) believes that tolerance should be scored from the threshold value rather than from the onset of stimulus. Gelfand's tolerance value indicates only the time that the subject is actually in pain.

Gelfand (11) also emphasized the importance 18 of determining threshold-tolerance relationships, noting that if a close relationship should exist studies could be concerned only with the variable of threshold, which is simpler and less noxious to measure. However, the relationship between pain threshold and tolerance seems to depend on the investigator's definition of tolerance. When tolerance

**19**    Strong implications of a cause-effect factor seem to be offered in this paragraph.  If the authors of reference 10 indeed have made such an inference, the
writer is obligated to offer further explanation.  Techniques of statistical correlation, which seem to be what are involved, do not ordinarily provide an
adequate basis for such assumptions.

is scored from onset of stimulation, toler-
ance-threshold relationships reflected by
correlation coefficients of .63, .72, .64 (5),
and .61, .68 (11), have been reported. When
the two variables are defined as independent
factors rather than as parts of a whole, low
relationships exist. Using the definition
of tolerance as maximum time minus threshold
time, threshold-tolerance relationships ranging from -.09 to .18 have been found (5, 12).

Threshold, in man, has been found to be
relatively stable and quite constant from
subject to subject, while tolerance is quite
variable (16, 24). There seems to be general
agreement that tolerance has a larger psychological component, whereas threshold is primarily physiological in nature. The psychological component is evidenced by the fact
that personality factors have been found to
be related to tolerance, but not to thresh-      **19**
old (10). Several authors (11, 38, 40) note
that tolerance can be affected by test in-

**20**     To what does the word "This" in the final sentence refer?  Collective
pronouns, particularly when employed at the close of a complicated paragraph, may have the effect of pointing at different antecedents for different
readers, or worse, at different antecedents for the author and the reader.  In
writing of this kind, clarity often demands the use of specific identifiers (key
words or phrases) rather than a pronoun, which may achieve economy at the
cost of accuracy.  Unless there is one and only one possible referent, it is
better to risk sounding stuffy through repetition than to risk leaving the
reader with "this," "that," "it," or "they," and a handful of antecedent
candidates.

structions to a much greater degree than can

threshold.   This again demonstrates the larger **20**

contribution of a psychological component to

pain tolerance.

### Factors Related to Pain Tolerance

Tissue damage and consequent release of

histamine partly explain pain sensation, but

in higher species the perception and toler-

ance of pain is not only a function of tissue

damage and presence of histamine.   Many re-

ports have been made of serious injuries being

almost unnoticed when occurring under stress-

ful conditions.   A linear relationship be-

tween stimulus intensity and the intensity

of pain felt cannot be demonstrated (27).

Previous experiences, perceptual type, and

motivation influence the amount of pain per-

ceived.   Eysenck (9) postulated that humans

differ with respect to the speed and strength

with which excitation and inhibition are

produced.   Individuals who slowly and weakly

**21**    It would have been useful if the author had made explicit the relevance of
this finding to the proposed study. It is easy to forget that patterns of reasoning that are so familiar as to seem obvious to the author may be obscure
for the reader on first encounter. Even when the importance of a particular
line of investigation has been specified, it is helpful to insert periodic reitera-
tions. This is particularly true in a long sequence of review that is unpunctu-
ated by discussion or summary.

generate excitatory potentials are predis-
posed to develop introverted patterns of behavior, while those who quickly and strongly
generate excitatory potentials are predis-
posed to develop extroverted patterns of
behavior. Using the Maudsly Personality In-
ventory and a radiant heat pain test, Lynn
and Eysenck (23) found a significant correlation of .69 with extroversion and pain
tolerance. As discussed earlier, Petrie (28)
classified subjects, in terms of modulation
of sensory experience, as reducers, moderators,
and augmentors. The reducer subjectively
decreases whatever is perceived, while the
augmenter increases. The reducer's higher
pain tolerance is explained in the following
way: the reduction of the perceived sensation of pain causes subsequent larger waves
of pain to be perceived as less intense (29).

As a measure of reduction, Petrie used es- **21**
timation of the size of blocks manipulated
by blindfolded subjects. The amount of re-

**22**  The work of Sweeney and Fine would be appropriate for inclusion in any critical review of work in the area but it does not appear to have more than an oblique bearing on the proposed study. Perhaps it could be included in a single summary sentence. For the novice researcher such judgments are difficult to make. There is the nagging fear that a knowledgeable advisor will note the omission and feel that the student has skipped over or even missed a portion of the literature. There also is the normal human instinct to display all the fruits of long and honest labor in the library. In the end, however, the simple question, "is this item really essential to the reader's understanding of my study?" must be applied in trimming the review down to size. There is more to lose in dulling the senses of the reader through over-inclusion than in the risk of being caught off base with an omission.

duction was correlated with pain tolerance
measures obtained by radiant heat (28).
Sweeney (34) and Dinnerstein et al. (8) generally supported this work, while Levine
et al. (21) failed to replicate the former
results. This failure might be due to differing methods of measurement: Levine et al.
increased the stimulus in discrete steps,
while the previous methods by Petrie and
Sweeney continuously increased the level of
pain.

Sweeney and Fine (35) related pain toler-   **22**
ance to field dependence, which they defined
as a continuum ranging from analytical perception where individual segments of the environment are perceived as distinct from
their background, to global perception where
the entire environmental structure is perceived. They found the global perceiver high
in pain tolerance, probably because he does
not focus on the most overwhelming aspect
(pain) in his environment. The pain is em-

**23**    Here the author could have been more concise in discussion of the relationships among age, experience, and pain.  Age and parent-child relationships
are of no direct concern in the proposed study.  Experience is relevant only
in that it includes athletic activity.  In such a complex domain as this it
always is tempting to leave the reader to sort out the implication for himself.  To do more than report the research seems to invite confusion.  This
particular buck, however, must always stop at the investigator's desk.  If the
author cannot identify a clear point that is tangent to the proposed study, he
is left with the question of why the material has been included at all.

bedded in his environmental structure and thus is perceived as less intense.

Early experience also may influence percep- **23** tion of pain. Collins (6) administered to subjects a childhood history questionnaire which measured the degree of early protection by parents as well as early independence from parents. Using electrical stimulation, he found a correlation of .67 between pain threshold and protection, and .38 between pain tolerance and protection. This was supported by a correlation of -.50 between threshold and independence, and -.32 between tolerance and independence. All correlations were significant at the .01 level, but none was high enough to be considered predictive. He believed that individuals who were protected from early pain experience had a higher tolerance to pain, since their limited experience with it made it appear less threatening. His theory is supported by a report that dogs brought up in isolation, deprived of sensory

**24**    The comment regarding female subjects is interesting. If certain traits of personality in females persistently differ from males, and pain tolerance is related to such traits, then what might be expected regarding male and female pain tolerance? In this fashion the reader will leap ahead to wonder what might be. Unfortunately, the author provides neither help in suggesting some alternative possibilities, nor any clue to the links developed between this literature and the final form of the proposed investigation. Although the Review of Related Literature is not intended as a forum for interesting speculations, it is the proper place to build a background of reasonable questions that will support the nature of the proposed study.

experiences in early life, were very slow to avoid the pain of electric shock (25).

Investigators (33) studying the effect of age on pain sensitivity to radiant heat found that sensitivity remained relatively constant until age 50, but showed a sharp decline after age 60. Hall and Stride (14) found the same relationship between age and radiant heat pain. They also found a lack of relationship between I.Q. and pain threshold, but a sig-nificantly (p=<.001) lower threshold for females than males. Voevodsky et al. (36) **24** found no significant sex difference in tol-erance, neither did McKenna (24), nor Haslam (17) with threshold, while Kennard (19) re-ported no sex difference in threshold, but a significant tolerance difference in males and females. Analysis of the pain stimulus in these five studies does not provide clari-fication of these discrepancies. The two studies finding a sex difference used elec-tric shock and radiant heat, while the three

**25**   After reading this sentence the reader immediately will wonder what happen-
ed to Group 2 (which also would be expected to focus on the pain stimulus).
Even though the treatment involved may have been irrelevant to the main
thread of argument (or the results simply not significant), it is unfair to leave
the reader hanging once the matter has been reported.

which found no significant difference used radiant heat and cold water.

## Pain Distraction

In a study utilizing various sensory cues to distract from or focus on the pain of ice water, Kanfer and Goldfoot (18) divided subjects into five groups: (1) Control; (2) Negative set, wherein the examiner described the pain to be expected; (3) Talk, in which the subject described his feelings from moment to moment; (4) Distraction (clock), wherein a clock was used by subjects to set goals for themselves; and (5) Distraction (slides), in which the subject manipulated a slide projector with the non-test hand and viewed slides. After the ice water test, subjects rated the pain on an ordinal scale ranging from 1-5. Groups 4 and 5 were superior in time in the water, while Group 3, 25 which had focused on the pain sensation, was

quite poor.  It was hypothesized that distraction competed with the pain sensation for
attention, and thus prolonged toleration.

Attempting to assess the worth of distraction in raising tolerance, one research team
(27) utilized both intense noise and a placebo
as distractors during an ice water test.
Finger immersion time was the pain measurement.  Several groups were formed, in which
the variables of noise, music, and experimenter suggestion were manipulated.  Auditory
stimuli plus experimenter suggestion that
pain would be lessened under auditory stimulus
conditions resulted in the most marked pain
tolerance increases.

Bandler et al. (1) hypothesized that perception of pain is partly an influence of
one's observation of his own response to the
stimulus.  He utilized electric shock under
three conditions:  (1) red light, push button
and shock will end; (2) green light, no escape; (3) yellow light, speed of button push

**26**    Given the description of the three conditions, can the reader be absolutely
sure which set of experimental conditions was applied to the "escape"
group? If the reader asks how the results relate to the hypothesis established
in the first sentence, will he now know enough to make an intelligent judgment? Finally, aside from the fact that it deals with the perception of pain,
what does the author think Bandler's work contributes to an understanding
of the proposed study? Only by asking such questions can the novice avoid
the kind of confusion apparent in this paragraph.

**27**    This quotation provides a useful instance for application of the two basic
rules governing direct use of another author's words. Does the weight of
particularly authoritative judgment or the unique nature of expression appear
to justify this quotation?

stressed, it might or might not end shock.
Subjects rated the painful shock, which was
the same for all conditions, from 1-7.  The
escape group rated the pain significantly        **26**
higher than the other groups.

Social justification is another factor that
affects subjects' tolerance for shock.
Zimbardo (41) had subjects learn a list of
words with associated shock.  Half of the
group was asked to participate in a second
experiment, in which the importance of the
research was stressed.  The other half of
the group was also asked to participate a
second time, but no reason was given.  The
group with justification for continuing reported less pain from the same stimulus intensity than the group that was given no
justification for continuing.  Engaging in
an activity viewed as worthwhile to the person seems to reduce the perceived pain involved with it.  As Brown (3:70) states,
"When one is engrossed in exciting or chal-        **27**

**28**     The point about the use of a motor task as a pain distractor should be
stressed, because it is one of the original and primary contributions of the
proposed study. Removing it from this summary paragraph and building an
independent paragraph to elaborate the point would serve to focus attention
on its relevance to the study.

lenging tasks, physical injury may be sustained and yet go completely unnoticed until the activities cease."

All of the studies reviewed report increased tolerance to pain when distractors of various types were introduced during the pain application. The attractiveness and challenge of the task appear to influence its efficiency as a distractor. No studies were reviewed in which the distractor was primarily a motor task, or in which the effect of the pain ap- **28** plication upon the performance of the distracting task was observed.

Pain Responses of
Athletes and Nonathletes

Ryan and Kovacic (32), using radiant heat to establish threshold measures, and gross pressure and muscle ischemia to establish tolerance measures, tested a non-athletic group, a non-contact sports athletic group,

**29**    The author has not suggested how this second study contributes to the understanding of pain tolerance. Further, the precise reason for including this small category (containing only two studies) has not been made explicit. For the reader to be aware that research has been conducted involving the pain responses of athletes and nonathletes is anything but a sufficient justification in itself. These studies do seem to link to other parts of the review (for example: Eysenck and Petrie) and there is some reason to suspect that they are related to the proposed study, but exactly how? Although particular details in the study need not be treated here, this is the point for building a foundation that will support later decisions.

and a contact sports athletic group. They
found no difference in the groups' thresholds, but significantly higher tolerance
values in the contact sport group than in the
non-contact athletic group. The non-contact
group had higher tolerance values than the
nonathletes, indicating a relationship between
willingness to tolerate pain and type of
athletic activity chosen. Ryan and Foster **29**
(31) replicated the results of Ryan and
Kovacic using high school boys. They also
measured reaction time, time estimation, and
kinesthetic after-effect of size estimation.
They found no significant difference in the
reaction time of the three groups, but there
were significant reductions in time and size
estimation by contact athletes. The non-
contact athletes were in the middle of the
continuum and the nonathletes were at the
opposite end.

Summary of Pain information

and Related Questions

Pain that individuals experience, measured largely by introspective report, has been analyzed in terms of threshold and tolerance levels. Pain threshold is that noxious stimulus value which gives rise to just noticeable pain, while pain tolerance is defined as the upper limit of pain an individual is willing to accept under experimental conditions. Threshold is relatively stable and constant in man, but tolerance values are considerably affected by psychological components.

Pain tolerance has been related to perceptual types, such as field dependent individuals, and it has been shown to relate to at least one personality trait--extroversion. Early experiences affect tolerance, in that those who are protected from early pain have higher tolerance levels. Motivation, in the form of appeals to individuals' social con-

**30**      The motivational factor of desire to win has not been sufficiently discussed
in the previous section to merit a summary statement of this order. Although
this sentence seems to relate to the points developed in the following paragraph, the entire matter of inhibiting pain stimuli by the athlete who is ab-
sorbed in the game outcome (and the logical relation of this process to the
construct of pain distraction) will be no more clear in this summary than it
was in the main text. What now is obvious is that the rationale for expecting
the athlete's absorption in the game to serve as a potential pain distractor
deserved much more discussion when the matter was first introduced in the
review of literature.

**31**      The summary of the related literature should systematically build a case for
the study. It should: (1) emphasize discrepancies in the literature that call
for questions included in the proposed study, (2) identify questions left unanswered by previous research, and (3) reach a logical climax with the statement of experimental hypotheses. The topics of this summary vascillate from
distractors to athletes, to sex differences, and back to distractors again. The
summary must build continuously until the reader is psychologically set, both
in terms of pertinent information and in terms of an affective need for logical
closure.

science, has had incrementing effects upon
tolerance levels.  The motivational factor        **30**
such as physical competition or desire to
win, as so often is seen in athletics, has
not been studied as a factor which might raise
pain tolerance levels.  Painful stimuli are
psychologically and systematically reduced or
augmented by some individuals, and athletes
have been found to be among those who systematically reduce pain stimuli.

Distractions, such as conversation, visual
stimuli, or auditory stimuli have the effect
of raising tolerance levels, perhaps because
the distractor competes with the pain sensation for attention.  Meeting the demands of
a neuromuscular skill task might also serve
as a distractor; yet, no investigator has
reported the use of a skill task as a distractor.

Male athletes tolerate more pain than non-      **31**
athletes, and contact sport athletes tolerate
more pain than non-contact sport athletes.

**32**    This is a typical personification of an inanimate object. A proposed study
cannot "hope" for anything. So far as we know, only humans have the capacity to hope, and certainly only a human could yearn to clarify the interactions between pain tolerance and neuromuscular performance. Personfica-
tion of inanimate objects is an error that occurs frequently in the research
literature – and not just that portion produced by novices. The ubiquitousness of the error does not justify its proliferation.

Male athletes have been shown to have at least one personality trait--extroversion--that relates to pain tolerance, and that might affect psychological pain apperception. If there is a general relationship between pain tolerance and athletic participation, one should be able to demonstrate it in females as well as in males. This knowledge would be useful in the construction of any predictive system.

The effectiveness of a neuromuscular skill as a distractor from painful stimuli has not been studied. Additionally, pain threshold and tolerance have not been studied in women subjects. The proposed study, by synthesizing general findings concerning pain tolerance, factors related to pain tolerance, distractors of pain, personality and perceptual relationship of pain, hopes to clarify to some **32** extent the interactions of pain tolerance and neuromuscular performance in female athletes and nonathletes.

**33**     It is not apparent that any particular part of the knowledge base provides
direct support for this hypothesis. Although *a priori* hypotheses may be developed through logic and the use of theory, they should be identified as
such.

## HYPOTHESES

To fulfill the purposes of the study, the
following hypotheses will be tested:

1.  The pain threshold of athletes will not    **33**
    be significantly different from that of
    the nonathletes.

2.  There will be no significant difference
    between athletes and nonathletes in
    psychological pain apperception.

3.  Pain tolerance will be greater for both
    athletes and nonathletes under conditions
    of distraction than under conditions of
    no distraction.

4.  Athletes will tolerate significantly more
    pain than nonathletes, under conditions
    of both distraction and non-distraction.

5.  The interaction between groups and condi-
    tions of distraction will be significant,
    in that athletes will allow themselves
    to be more distracted by the neuromuscular
    task and will tolerate more pain.

**34**     This proposal would be strengthened if a section titled "Importance of the Proposed Study" were included following the hypotheses. From a reading of the hypotheses the reader will have sensed that the study will have potential contributions for both basic knowledge and practice. If a proper foundation has been laid, aggressive speculation that makes explicit some of the study's implications will not be an unreasonable method of encouraging the reader's further attention. Such a short section might pursue the points suggested below.

If pain tolerance is significantly greater in athletes — not only in males but in females — it is conceivable that this type of measure could be included in a battery of other independent variables to predict athletic success. Pain tolerance assessment might become a significant component in an athletic-personality profile scale, or it might be used in counseling athletes regarding appropriate sports for them to pursue.

In addition, if pain threshold is significantly different in athletes and non-athletes, and it also is highly correlated to pain tolerance, then measures of pain threshold could be substituted for pain tolerance measures in a test battery used to select athletes.

If physical distraction serves to increase signficantly the amount of pain to be tolerated, then physical educators could devise different types of distractors to be used in conjunction with painful endurance work. Knowledge about an interaction between pain tolerance and distraction would contribute to the knowledge base of sport psychology.

The relationship of pain apperception, as revealed by a psychological paper and pencil test, to pain tolerance would constitute a contribution to the body of scientific knowledge concerning pain factors. In addition, it would be of practical importance if researchers could substitute a paper and pencil test for painful stimuli in experimental data collection situations.

**35**     As there is a difficult point concerning the uniformity of the subject group, it would be wise to note the fact that Typical Junior College plays in national tournaments and that the team in question is recognized as an exceptionally skilled group.

**36**     These subjects, being volunteers, automatically limit the generalizability of the study. The reader will wonder at once why the author has not considered the possibility of drawing a random sample of nonathlete females in the college.

**37**     Given the nature of college physical education classes and undergraduate student populations as a whole, it would be wise to present plans for handling subject mortality.

6. No significant relationship exists between any two or more variables of psychological pain apperception, pain threshold, pain tolerance, and distracted tolerance.

**34**

## PROCEDURES

### Subjects

Forty-eight women enrolled either at Western State College or at Typical Junior College with no restrictions on physical activity will serve as subjects for this investigation. Twenty-four of the subjects will be selected as a sample from a population of athletic college women, on the basis of their membership on the basketball teams from Typical Junior College **35** and from Western State College. These teams were selected because they both had winning seasons. An equivalent number of women enrolled at Western State College will serve as a control group. These students, all of whom **36** have no restrictions of their physical acti- **37**

**38**     A note should be provided here concerning informed consent, and specimen
forms should be included in the Appendix.

**39**     From what studies are these reliabilities derived? It would be helpful to include some magnitudes of amperes so that the reader will have an idea of the
range involved in the study. This information is necessary because the proposal will have to be accepted by a campus Committee for Rights of Human
Subjects. The Committee members should be able to tell whether the range
to be employed lies within the range that the literature suggests to be
"normal and appropriate." The rationale for the 30 ma maximum should receive specific discussion.

**40**     Reference to the pilot study is a sound tactic. An additional statement indicating that the pilot study results may be found in the Appendix will lend
even more weight to the argument.

vity, will be volunteers from required physical
education classes.

**38**

## Equipment

Pain Test. Pain will be administered in the
form of a direct current produced by a chronaximeter, Teca Model CH-3. Reliabilities of **39**
.81 for threshold and .91 for tolerance measures have been reported by investigators who
used instruments of this type. The investigator used this instrument in a pilot study
and obtained within-day reliabilities of .96 **40**
(N = 29) for tolerance measurements. In the
proposed study, direct electrical current will
be used with a one ma/sec. increase in intensity to a maximum output of 30 ma.

Electrical stimulus was selected as the
producer of pain in this study, as it has been
shown to be more accurately controlled, more
sharply localized, and of shorter duration
than other types of stimuli (2). All quali-

**41**    The reader who is unfamiliar with psychophysical tests will have no idea how this task is performed. A simple descriptive sentence concerning the task would make the entire paragraph more meaningful. For example, the importance of timing stylus contact with the side of the hole will be lost on the reader unless he can visualize the task. Although the reference to the pilot study is appropriate, the reader still will be unaware of what criteria were used to decide which hole diameter provided "a suitable range of scores." Finally, no rationale is provided for using this particular task as a distractor. There should be some specific reasons for the choice and these should be made explicit.

ties of pain can be produced and reproducible values can be obtained. The stimulus can be expressed in standard physical units. The stimulation may be easily and rapidly applied. Identification of pain by subjects is easily accomplished.

Distraction Task. The distraction task will consist of performance on an electric steadiness test. A Hole Type Steadiness Tester, manufactured by the Lafayette Instrument Company will be utilized. This devise contains nine holes of varying sizes. The size of the hole to be used was determined by prior investigation, to provide a suitable range of scores. A Universal Timer will be wired to the circuit to record error time, that is, the amount of time, in milliseconds, that the stylus is in **41** contact with the side of the hole in which it is inserted. The Universal Timer, from Meylan Stopwatch Corporation, is a synchronous motor-driven instrument suitable for both automatic interval timing and elapsed time indication.

**42**    The Pain Apperception Test should be included in the Appendix, and a notation should be made here to that effect.

<u>Pain Apperception Test.</u>   The pain appercep-   **42**

tion test devised by Petrovich (30) will be

used.   This test was designed to consider the

psychological or emotional reactions of indi-

viduals to pain.   It is a series of 17 pictures

of painful or potentially painful situations,

wherein subjects rate each picture on an ordi-

nal scale with units ranging from 1-7 on pain

intensity and duration.   This test is based

on the premise that individuals tend to per-

ceive pain in others in a particular and rather

constant manner as a result of their experi-

ences and reactions regarding pain.   Petrovich

reported a split-half reliability estimate of

.70 for pain intensity and .84 for pain dura-

tion when the test was administered to female

subjects.   The test may be quickly and easily

administered to a group or an individual.


## Testing Procedures

This study will be conducted during the

**43**     It is not clear whether this is the recommended form of administration as suggested by Petrie, or a special variation devised to meet the particular needs of the proposed study.

**44**     Given this series of apparently arbitrary decisions, a host of questions will occur to the reader. Why two trials? Why not one, or ten? Why select the higher of the two trial results to denote threshold? Why not employ the lower of the two? These same questions must, at some point, have occurred to the author. The purpose of preparing a proposal is to communicate the author's resolution of such questions so that a fair and expert appraisal can be made of the proposed testing procedure. Here, that fundamental purpose of the proposal has been more confounded than served.

spring semester, 1969, at the Western State College and Typical Junior College campuses. Testing will be individualized, requiring approximately 30 minutes per subject and will begin with administration of the Pain Apperception Test.

PAT Administration. The pictures of the **43** PAT will be placed in a notebook so that the subject can determine the rate of viewing. Subjects will rate each picture on an ordinal scale ranging from one to seven for pain intensity and for pain duration.

Pain Threshold Testing. Following the rating of the PAT stimulus pictures, pain thresholds for the preferred arm will be secured. Recordings will be in milliamps. Subjects will be seated at a table, so that their preferred arm is resting on the table in a position of supination. The stimulating electrodes will be placed on the ulnar nerve, just rostral to the elbow, medial aspect. Two trials will be ad- **44** ministered, the higher of the two scores de-

**45**     A complete transcript of all subject instructions should be included in the Appendix and noted here.

**46**     The first two sentences in this paragraph relate to overall testing procedure, rather than to the specific administration of the pain tolerance test. These two sentences would be more appropriate if they were expanded to include all the tests and were presented as the second paragraph under the subtitle "Testing Procedures."

noting threshold. Subjects are to indicate     **45**

with a verbal signal as soon as the sensation

becomes one that they judge to be painful.

Pain Tolerance Administration. Pain toler-     **46**

will be measured under two conditions, dis-

traction and no distraction; order of condi-

tions to be rotated among subjects. One half

of each group will be randomly assigned to

undergo the tolerance condition first. In

this condition, the experimenter will apply

the chronaximeter electrode to the skin sur-

face immediately over the ulnar nerve and in-

crease the current intensity one ma/sec. to

a maximum output of 30 ma. The pain toler-

ance criterion measure will be the highest

intensity that the subject will allow before

requesting that the current be terminated.

Distracted Pain Tolerance Administration.

The criterion measure for Distracted Pain

Tolerance will be the highest intensity in

milliamps that the subject will allow while

she is completing the steadiness task. During

**47**     This is the appropriate point to include a full review of the experimental
design proposed for the study. A separate section (using the same order of
subheading as Testing Procedures) should be inserted before the section on
Statistical Analysis. The explanation should include both attention to the
basic model, a single factor with repeated measures design, and the particular
permutation proposed for this study, two fixed factors with replication of
measures on one factor. A simple diagram would be a useful aid for many
readers. The order of test administration also should be clarified in this section. Finally a concluding explanatory note should link the particular groups
of data derived from the test administration to the major means of analysis to
be discussed in the next section (simple analysis of variance in combination
with correlational analysis).

this condition, the subject's preferred arm will be placed, as described for threshold measures, on the table. The Steadiness Tester will be placed at fingertip distance when the subject's arm is placed on the table, elbow on the edge, forming a 90° angle with the edge. The stylus will be held between the thumb and the first two fingers, within two inches of its distal end, and will be inserted into the proper hole when the test begins. No part of the subject's body may touch the table during the test. The length of the test will be 30 seconds. The subject will be told that the error time per five seconds will be re-corded, and that she should make every attempt to perform well on the steadiness test. Sec-onds will be counted off on a tape recorder, Channel Master, model 6464.

**47**

## Statistical Analyses

Frequency distributions of pain threshold, tolerance, distracted tolerance, and appercep-

**48**  This point raises the obvious question "What will be done in the event of skewed or kurtotic deviations?" Here it is essential to note whether distributions proved to be normal in the pilot study.

tion will be described by the utilization of program DISTAT, which provides means, standard deviations, and coefficients indicating the kurtosis and skewness of the distributions.   **48**

The test order of the two pain conditions, distracted vs. non-distracted, will be subjected to an analysis of variance. If the variance due to an interaction effect between test order and testing condition is not significantly different from zero, the error terms for the order groups will be pooled, and the analyses described below will be compiled using all subjects regardless of test order. If the order of testing significantly affects the tolerance scores, the following analyses will be computed for each order group.

A one-way analysis of variance will be completed to determine whether pain thresholds of athletes are significantly different from those of nonathletes (Hypothesis 1). An example of the table to be produced as a result of this analysis is appended to the proposal.

Hypotheses 2, 3, and 4 refer not only to differences between athletes and nonathletes, but also to differences within each subject's response to a distracted or non-distracted condition. This represents a two-factor experiment with repeated measures, in which the between factor is athletic vs. nonathletic status, while the within factor is the distracted vs. non-distracted condition of measurement. The computer program AVAR 23 will be used to complete this analysis. The table to be produced is appended to the proposal.

Finally, a correlation matrix will be obtained by using program MAXFAC in which Pearson product-moment coefficients among each of the variables of the study are computed (Hypothesis 5).

**49**     The presentation of the proposed figure provides the reader with a reinforced and vivid understanding of hypotheses. It serves the additional function of providing evidence that the author has carefully calculated both the nature and the presentation of the results to be obtained. A graphic illustration such as Figure 1 may also serve as a stimulus for questioning method; for instance, is the distraction variable really a continuum, as implied in this figure? If it is not a continuum, is this type of figure appropriate?

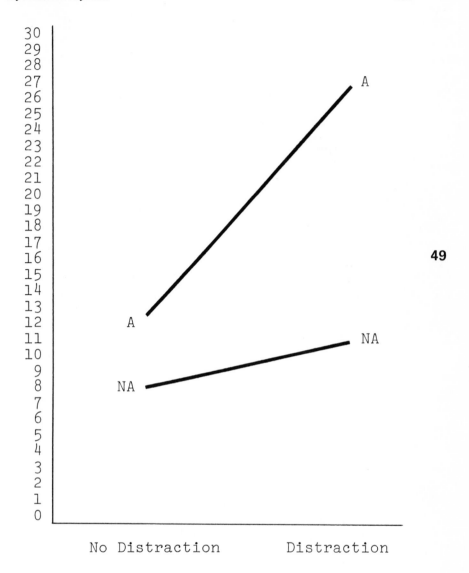

**49**

FIGURE 1

PAIN TOLERANCE IN ATHLETES AND NON-
ATHLETES UNDER CONDITIONS OF DIS-
TRACTION AND NON-DISTRACTION.

**50**   The presentation of both Tables I and II provides the function of displaying the ANOVA models to be used. A cursory glance at the variables to be analyzed, the sources of variance, and the degrees of freedom will better enable the reader to evaluate the appropriateness of the analyses. Once again, the preparation of these tables relieves the author of making such display decisions when the results become available. When an author is able simply to insert values in a previously prepared table, it is possible to move immediately to the interpretation stage of the project while the excitement of having obtained the results is still high.

TABLE I

ANALYSIS OF VARIANCE ATTRIBUTABLE TO
DIFFERENCES IN PAIN THRESHOLD AND
PAIN APPERCEPTION OF ATHLETES
AND NON-ATHLETES

**50**

| Variable | Source of Variance | MS | df | $F$ Value |
|----------|--------------------|----|----|-----------|
| Pain Threshold | Total | | | |
| | Between | | 2 | |
| | Within | | | |
| Pain Apperception | Total | | | |
| | Between | | 2 | |
| | Within | | | |

TABLE II

ANALYSIS OF VARIANCE ATTRIBUTABLE TO
ATHLETIC STATUS AND CONDITIONS
OF DISTRACTION

| Source of Variation | Mean Square | df | $F$ ratio |
|---------------------|-------------|----|-----------|
| Total | | 95 | |
| Between subjects | | 47 | |
|   Groups[a] | | 1 | * |
|   Subjects within groups | | 46 | |
| Within subjects | | 48 | |
|   Conditions[b] | | 1 | * |
|   Groups X conditions | | 1 | * |
|   Conditions X subjects | | | |
|     within groups | | 46 | |

*With df = 1/46, and F ratio > 4.02 = $p < .05$.
[a]Groups = 2; Athletes or non-athletes
[b]Conditions = 2; Distracted or nondistracted

**51**     Intercorrelations to be obtained are clearly presented by this table. Although
the degrees of freedom may change as a result of subject mortality, all that
remains upon data analysis is insertion of the resultant values. Again, important questions may be evoked as a result of viewing expected tables. What,
for example, is the importance of correlating distracted tolerance and pyscho-
logical pain apperception?   No mention or rationale to this has previously
been made.

TABLE III

CORRELATION COEFFICIENTS
AMONG PAIN VARIABLES                              **51**

| Variable | 2 | 3 | 4 | Mean | SD |
|---|---|---|---|---|---|
| 1.  Psychological Pain Apperception | – | – | – | -- | -- |
| 2.  Pain Threshold | | – | – | -- | -- |
| 3.  Pain Tolerance | | | – | -- | -- |
| 4.  Distracted Tolerance | | | | -- | -- |

With df = 46, an r > .30 = p < .05

REFERENCES

1. Bandler, R. J., G. R. Madaras, and D. J. Bem. "Self-Observation as a Source of Pain Perception." Journal of Personality and Social Psychology, 9:205-209, June 1968.

2. Bishop, G. H. "The Peripheral Unit for Pain." Journal of Neurophysiology, 7:71-80, January 1944.

3. Brown, Judson S. "Theoretical Note, A Behavioral Analysis of Masochism." Journal of Experimental Research in Personality, 1:65-70, March 1965.

4. Casey, Kenneth L. "Unit Analysis of Nociceptive Mechanisms in the Thalamus of the Awake Squirrel Monkey." Journal of Neurophysiology, 29:727-750, July 1966.

5. Clark, James W. and Dalbir Bindra. "Individual Differences in Pain Thresholds." Canadian Journal of Psychology, 10:69-76, June 1956.

6. Collins, L. G. "Pain Sensitivity and Ratings of Childhood Experience." Perceptual and Motor Skills, 21:349-350, October 1965.

7. Dallenbach, Karl M. "Pain: History and Present Status." American Journal of Psychology, 52:331-347, July 1939.

8. Dinnerstein, A. J. et al. "Pain Tolerance and Kinesthetic After-Effect." Perceptual and Motor Skills, 15:247-250, August 1962.

9. Eysenck, H. J. The Dynamics of Anxiety and Hysteria. New York: Frederick A. Praeger, 1957.

10. Gelfand, D. M., Sidney Gelfand, and M. W. Rardin. "Some Personality Factors Associated with Placebo Responsivity." Psychological Reports, 17:555-562, October 1965.

11. Gelfand, Sidney. "The Relationship of Experimental Pain Tolerance to Pain Threshold." Canadian Journal of Psychology, 18:36-42, March 1964.

12. Gelfand, Sidney, L. P. Ulmann, and Leonard Krasner. "The Placebo Response: An Experimental Approach." Journal of Nervous and Mental Disease, 136:379-387, April 1963.

13. Guyton, Arthur C. Textbook of Medical Physiology. Philadelphia: W. B. Saunders Company, 1966.

14. Hall, K. R. L. and E. Stride. "The Varying Response to Pain in Psychiatric Disorders: A Study in Abnormal Psychology." British Journal of Medical Psychology, 27:48-60, March 1954.

15. Hardy, James D., Harold G. Wolff, and Helen Goodell. Pain Sensations and Reactions. Baltimore: The Williams and Wilkins Co., 1952.

16. Hardy, James D., Harold G. Wolff, and Helen Goodell. "The Pain Threshold in Man." American Journal of Psychiatry, 99:744-751, March 1943.

17. Haslam, Diana R. "The Influence of Stimulus Scale-Interval Upon the Assessment of Pain Threshold." Quarterly Journal of Experimental Psychology, 17:65-68, February 1965.

18. Kanfer, F. H. and D. A. Goldfoot. "Self-Control and Tolerance of Noxious Stimulation." Psychological Reports, 18:79-85, February 1965.

19.  Kennard, Margaret A.  "The Response to Painful Stimuli of Patients with Severe Chronic Painful Conditions." Journal of Clinical Investigation, 31:245-252, March 1952.

20.  Langley, L. L.  Outline of Physiology. New York: McGraw-Hill Book Company, 1961.

21.  Levine, Fredric M., Bernard Tursky, and David C. Nichols.  "Tolerance for Pain, Extraversion and Neuroticism: Failure to Replicate Results." Perceptual and Motor Skills, 23:847-850, December 1966.

22.  Livingston, W. K.  "What is Pain?" Scientific American, 188:59-66, March 1953.

23.  Lynn, R. and H. J. Eysenck.  " Tolerance for Pain, Extraversion and Neuroticism." Perception and Motor Skills, 12:161-162, April 1961.

24.  McKenna, A. E.  "The Experimental Approach to Pain." Journal of Applied Physiology, 13:449-456, November 1958.

25.  Melzack, Ronald and T. H. Scott.  "The Effects of Early Experience on the Response to Pain." Journal of Comparative and Physiological Psychology, 50:155-161, April 1957.

26.  Melzack, Ronald and P. D. Wall.  "Pain Mechanisms: A New Theory." Science, 150:971-978, November 1965.

27.  Melzack, Ronald, A. Z. Weisz and L. T. Sprague.  "Stratagems for Controlling Pain: Contributions of Auditory Stimulation and Suggestion." Experimental Neurology, 8:239-247, September 1963.

28.  Petrie, Asenath.  Individuality in Pain and Suffering. Chicago: The University of Chicago Press, 1967.

29. Petrie, Asenath, Walter Collins and Philip Solomon. "The Tolerance for Pain and for Sensory Deprivation." American Journal of Psychology, 73:80-90, March 1960.

30. Petrovich, Donald V. "The Pain Apperception Test: Psychological Correlates of Pain Perception." Journal of Clinical Psychology, 14:367-374, October 1958.

31. Ryan, E. Dean and Robert Foster. "Athletic Participation and Perceptual Augmentation and Reduction." Journal of Personality and Social Psychology, 6:472-476, August 1967.

32. Ryan, E. Dean and Charles R. Kovacic. "Pain Tolerance and Athletic Participation." Perceptual and Motor Skills, 22:383-390, April 1966.

33. Schludermann, E. and J. P. Zubek. "Effect of Age on Pain Sensitivity." Perceptual and Motor Skills, 22:383-390, April 1966.

34. Sweeney, Donald R. "Pain Reactivity and Kinesthetic Aftereffect." Perceptual and Motor Skills, 22:763-769, June 1966.

35. Sweeney, Donald R. and B. J. Fine. "Pain Reactivity and Field Dependence." Perceptual and Motor Skills, 21:757-758, December 1965.

36. Voevodsky, John et al. "The Measurement of Suprathreshold Pain." American Journal of Psychology, 80:124-128, March 1967.

37. Wolff, B. Berthold. "The Relationship of Experimental Pain Tolerance to Pain Threshold: A Critique of Gelfand's Paper." Canadian Journal of Psychology, 18:249-253, September 1964.

38. Wolff, B. Berthold and A. A. Horland.
    "Effect of Suggestion upon Experimental
    Pain: A Validation Study." Journal of
    Abnormal Psychology, 72:403-407, October
    1967.

39. Wolff, B. Berthold and Murray E. Jarvik.
    "Relationship between Superficial and
    Deep Somatic Thresholds of Pain with a
    Note on Handedness." American Journal
    of Psychology, 77:589-599, December 1964.

40. Wolff, B. Berthold, N. A. Krasnegor and
    R. S. Farr. "Effect of Suggestion upon
    Experimental Pain Response Parameters."
    Perceptual and Motor Skills, 21:675-683,
    December 1965.

41. Zimbardo, P. D. et al. "Control of Pain
    Motivation by Cognitive Dissonance."
    Science, 151:217-219, January 1966.

## PROPOSAL NUMBER 2
## INTRODUCTORY NOTE

The following proposal differs from the preceeding specimen in three important respects. First, the stage of development represented is earlier in the total process of devising a research plan, being intermediate with respect to the two flanking proposals. In most graduate departments, this document would represent a first draft produced for preliminary advice and critical feedback. Second, the kind of research involved — a field-based program evaluation study — differs in ways that are both substantial and subtle. Third, in contrast to those in the preceding specimen, the more important flaws represented in this proposal are complex problems of design, difficult considerations of conceptual definition, and technical questions related to instrument validation and reliability, rather than concerns related to organization and effective communication of ideas. With a few necessary exceptions, the accompanying discussion of the proposal will not provide extensive advice for improving design and method; standard references in the research literature are the proper source for such remediation. The discussion will focus instead on the document itself as the vehicle within which issues of design and method must be resolved and communicated to a critical audience.

**1**     As used in the title, the phase "Effect . . . On Improving . . . " not only is
poor usage but presumes a result to be obtained from the study: that improvement *will be demonstrated.*   Simply dropping the word "improving"
leaves a sound if incomplete title.   The fact that the subject population consists entirely of children "who exhibit perceptual-motor difficulties" seems to
warrant some note in the title.

EFFECT OF A CHILDREN'S

DEVELOPMENTAL CLINIC ON IMPROVING     **1**

SELECTED PERCEPTUAL-MOTOR ATTRIBUTES


A Thesis Proposal


Presented to

the Faculty of Graduate Studies

School of Physical Education

Erehwon University


In Partial Fulfillment

of the Requirements for the Degree

Master of Science


by

A Graduate Student

January 1974

**2**     In this context the clinic is not a "type of program" but simply a program, the one under discussion. With an abstraction such as "the clinic" it is best to avoid attributing animate actions such as "attempts." To say that the clinic provides a setting is sufficient.

**3**     The need for program evaluation, not the additional functions of the clinic, should be stressed in this paragraph. The fact that the clinic also offers opportunities for field experiences and other types of research activities is irrelevant to this study and should not consume a third of the introduction.

INTRODUCTION

The Children's Developmental Clinic at
Erehwon Unversity is a type of support pro-      2
gram for children with special needs (Lord,
1973).  It attempts to provide a setting
which may assist children who exhibit perceptual-motor difficulties.  The physical
activity approach of the clinic may help
children to: (a) achieve success and enjoy-
ment in a play and movement setting; (b) gain
increasing self-confidence in their bodies
and what they can do with them; (c) improve
basic perceptual-motor skills in a variety
of areas; (d) improve physical fitness.

The clinic also serves two other functions.      3
It offers opportunities for physical education and special education students to experience working with exceptional children,
as well as for research hypotheses to be ex-
plored concerning exceptional children, physical activity, and motor development.  Even

**4**    The student author is likely to make a sensitive reader uneasy with the sweeping assertion that "it is probable that clinics. . . do aid children." Whether they produce a significant difference is the very question under investigation in the proposed study. Even though previous studies examined in the background review may provide some ground for the assertion, this study will focus on one particular clinic, which may or may not reflect such a wider tendency. Any hint, even inadvertent, of prejudgment is inappropriate.

**5**    The primary purpose of this study is to evaluate a program; yet even the pragmatic questioning of the value of an operational program must have a basic rationale, and this rationale is not presented in the introduction to the proposal. The principal function of this introduction should not be an introduction to the clinic, its purposes, and other activities related to it, but rather, an introduction to the effects the clinic is expected to produce in its clients and generally how the program is designed to generate these outcomes. The "why" of the expected effects of the clinic should then later justify the selection of tests, subject groups, and application of the experimental treatment.

**6**    The problem as stated here is ambiguous. Although testable hypotheses are not required in the statement of the problem, the statement must be explicit in terms of what is to be done. What is meant by the words "aid" and "improvement" in this statement? Do we expect to find a media, social, administrative, or physical aid? What behavior, and how much change, will be accepted as improvement? The statement of the problem should provide an obvious lead into the later discussion of testable questions or formal hypotheses. In addition, ordinary usage for the generic construct "perceptual-motor" does not include strength, power, body part awareness, or gross agility. In their most simple form of expression these latter attributes do not involve important components of conscious perception. Does the author really mean "perceptual *and* motor" attributes?

though it is probable that clinics such as **4**

these do aid children in developing percep-

tual-motor skills to some extent, it is nec-

essary to determine objectively the nature of

the effects and to explain them. A detailed,

systematic approach is needed for a total

evaluation of the clinic program. Looking

at perceptual-motor improvement is a beginning

in the long list of research questions which

have evolved in relation to the clinic. **5**

## The Problem

Does the Children's Developmental Clinic **6**

aid children in improving the basic perceptual-

motor attributes of strength, body part aware-

ness, balance, gross agility, eye-hand coordi-

nation, power, and timing?

## Importance of the Problem

Previous researchers have evaluated chil-

dren's clinical programs and found signifi-

cant changes in specific perceptual-motor

skills and development (Johnson, 1967; Fretz,

**7**     What is intended by the allusion to "other types" of programs? What type(s) did the Johnson studies evaluate? Is it possible that the author intends only the simple observation that some evaluations produce evidence of positive program impact, whereas others do not? If so, the point can be made with less confusion.

**8**     "Tended to view negatively" is an inappropriate way to characterize research results. Either there were negative results or there were not. If the results vary with the criterion measure employed (or the confidence level established), then that is the point to be made. If six out of ten studies produced nonsignificance, then that is the point to be made. Ambiguities such as "tended" tell the reader nothing useful about the research.

**9**     Is the referrent of "these programs" only those producing negative results, or does it include Johnson's studies? Further, how do the studies of O'Connor and Falik differ from the studies of Mann, and Goodman and Hammill? Is the intended distinction that of criteria employed or results obtained, or both?

**10**    What "theoretical aspects" does the author have in mind here? A difference in the dependent variables between several studies does not qualify as a matter of theory.

**11**    Here the paragraph begins to run on into a wholly new thought, already discussed on the previous page, about the importance of the problem. By now it is unclear whether the author thinks the main importance of the study is provided by resolving conflicting research findings, or by evaluating the clinic's program.

**12**    Here another subject is broached for this already overburdened paragraph. This topic appears to demand both status as a separate paragraph and more careful explication. If the proposed study simply differs from that undertaken by Fretz, Johnson, and Johnson, in what sense does the author think it will be "unique"? The reader already has been informed that Fretz, Johnson, and Johnson employed measures of "specific perceptual-motor skills and development." The author of the proposal announces, however, that he will be unique by employing "basic measures" of perceptual-motor skills and by following Cratty's injunction to give priority to motor development. If a rose by another name is not to smell the same, the subtle distinctions must be made with far greater care than has been employed here.

**13**    Either as English usage or as a logical proposition, the proposal that "the evaluation . . . will attempt to measure . . . skills" will distress most readers. The author performs the labors of measurement, not an abstraction such as "the evaluation." Here, as elsewhere throughout the proposal, the passive voice ("the attributes will be measured") could serve to avoid reference either to the author or to inappropriate abstractions. Finally, if the measures prove inadequate, the study will have to be revised or abandoned, hence the word "attempt" serves no purpose.

Johnson, & Johnson, 1969). There have been
many evaluations of other types of percep-      7
tual-motor training and development programs
which have tended to view negatively the        8
effectiveness of the programs (Mann, 1970;
Goodman & Hammill, 1973). In most cases,
however, these programs have been used and       9
evaluated on the basis that they develop
reading readiness, improve intellectual functioning, or predict those children who have
learning disabilities (O'Conner, 1969; Falik,
1969). Thus one can only speculate on the
program effectiveness due to the controversial
nature of the theoretical aspects. An eval-     10
uation is essential for the clinic to determine whether the perceptual-motor improvement    11
objective is being met. The evaluation will
be unique when compared to the study by Fretz,   12
Johnson, and Johnson in that it will attempt
to measure basic perceptual-motor skills. As    13
suggested by Cratty (1970), there is a need
to demonstrate motor development before pro-

**14**  It will be the children who demonstrate gains, not the clinic. "Positive gains in improvement" is a redundant statement that says, upon analysis, very little. It should be remembered that either negative or positive results of any study may prove to be a fruitful basis upon which more research may be developed.

**15**  The paragraph begins to run on at this point about the appropriateness of this particular research setting. Although this may have meaning to the researcher, it does not relate to the importance of the problem.

**16**  The final two sentences in this paragraph clearly must be cast into a separate paragraph and more clearly developed. The attentive reader immediately will begin to puzzle about the relationship of the point being made here and the point(s) made in the long preceding paragraph. If indeed the proposed study is unique in the range and sophistication of measures involved — and certainly this would support the argument being made for the importance of the study — then the matter demands much more specific attention and careful explanation than has been provided here. The reader already will have guessed that most of the preceding studies have used multiple measures. What exactly, then, will be the special advantage of the proposed study? The author seems to suggest that the advantage rests somehow in the nature of the instruments selected rather than in sheer numbers, but this point is never clarified.

ceeding toward speculation concerning other
benefits of the program.

If the clinic program demonstrates positive     **14**
gains in perceptual-motor improvement then
this could form a basis upon which more research concerning exceptional children, play,
and physical activity could be developed.  No
improvement in perceptual-motor attributes
may require a close examination of the clinic
objectives and program.  The clinic is ideal     **15**
for conducting research on play and motor
development because of its unique laboratory
status.  This study is also an attempt to
look at a wide range of perceptual-motor
attributes which appear to be involved in a
child's functioning.  Much of the research     **16**
on perceptual-motor theory has concerned itself with using tests which appear to evaluate
total perceptual-motor development but really
only measure a very few of its attributes.

**17**     The distinction between delimitations and limitations seems blurred here. Delimitations ordinarily include the conditions imposed by the researcher. They are necessary restrictions growing out of a particular set of circumstances. Items 1 and 2 under limitations ordinarily would be called delimitations. Consequent restrictions on the utility of the research, such as its generalizability, usually are noted under the heading of "limitations." The two categories appear to be reversed here.

**18**     The phrase "may be able" is inappropriate when used with the noun "change." Readers will wonder what "theory" was generated from previous studies. If the relevance of results from the proposed study to a pre-existing body of theoretical propositions is a major consideration in the design, then the reader has cause to anticipate some hint of it in the Introduction and a full discussion of it in the Review of Related Literature. In fact, there is no mention of theoretical rationale at all in either section. Is this just a careless bit of overly enthusiastic writing, or do we have evidence of a serious failure to come to grips with the problem to be investigated?

**19**     This is not a limitation, although it might be considered a delimitation. Delimitations ordinarily are considered to be those implacable facts of life the researcher chooses to accept because nothing can be done. In confronting this particular problem, the author has recourse to several useful (if imperfect) responses in the form of the design and analysis proposed.

## Delimitations

Specific results of this study may only be **17** applicable to the groups of children involved, but significant changes and trends may be able **18** to support theory generated from previous findings in children's clinical work.

## Limitations

The study will be limited:

(1) to those children who apply to be in-
    volved in the clinic program.

(2) by a lack of control on the amount of
    experience the child receives outside
    the clinic.

(3) in the analysis due to the non-equiva- **19**
    lence of groups.

## Definition of Terms

<u>Perceptual-motor attributes</u> -- for the pur-
pose of this study perceptual-motor attributes refers to the specific attributes of

**20**    The use of a string of references to support this point will be superfluous for
most readers.  If references are to be employed, however, it would be best to
use one or several of the "classic" studies that lie at the core of the child development literature.  At the least this would assure the knowledgeable reader
that the author is aware of basic reference material, as distinct from having
simply skimmed off several recent and obvious items from a bibliography. Additionally, in an abbreviated summary of related literature such as this, the literature related to developmental aspects of motor behavior is tangential at
best.  The literature critical to this study is that supporting short-term
changes in perceptual and motor behavior.  Much of the cited work presents
or refers to longitudinal studies, a category of investigation that is designed to
answer a set of questions not entirely related to those proposed in this study.

strength, body part awareness, balance, gross agility, eye-hand coordination, power, and timing.

Review of Related Literature

It is well documented that children progress through developmental stages in perceptual-motor efficiency (Espenshade & Eckert, **20** 1967; Cratty & Martin, 1969; Cratty, 1970). Most children are able to progress developmentally in chronological age group categories. Some children, however, such as those with learning disabilities or perceptual-motor deficits, lag behind their peers (Pyfer & Carlson, 1972). Several researchers have indicated (Johnson & Fretz, 1967; Fretz, Johnson, & Johnson, 1969; Cratty, 1970; Johnson, 1972) that support programs such as clinics may provide an opportunity for children to improve in areas such as perceptual-motor skills and thus be better able to relate and interact with their peers. It has also

**21**     Gains in confidence, improvement (never "increase") in self-concepts, and en-
hancement of success in other areas are ouside the question proposed for
study.   This is another clear indication that the problem to be examined is
not yet well defined.

**22**     No typological division of clinic "types" has been provided and the reader
should not be sent scurrying back to search for what will not be found. Both
of the sentences in this paragraph contain awkward constructions: "give
*support that* these" and "have, however, been critical as to the effectiveness
of the *programs meeting* their objectives."   Also, it is the authors rather than
the studies who would have been critical of clinic programs.   Further, the
word "critical" implies a level of action very different from that ordinarily
taken in a research report.   The author should be sure that criticism actually
is involved, as distinct from the simple act of reporting nonsignificant results.
Finally, the substance of this paragraph is redundant, having already been
noted.   More to the point here would be an examination of the differences
between the programs studied and the criteria for effectiveness employed.
As was suggested in the section of this monograph dealing with the review of
literature, it is this act of sorting and categorizing what is known, and the
tools for knowing, that constitutes the central creative act for many proposals.   It is from this key point that the design formulated for the present study
must take its genesis.

**23**     Here the author has misunderstood the proposal task.   The proper question is
not "where" the attributes were found, but "what" were the grounds for
their selection?   Combining the criterion of frequency of citation with an
ambiguous standard of importance provides little that is logical or persuasive
for the reader.   Once again the absence of a rationale, not only for the study
but for the operation of the clinic, is a defect that leaves the developing plan
to drift without an anchor.   As suggested both by this inadequacy and by
those identified in the discussion above, this section of the proposal must be
expanded in the next draft not simply to span a more inclusive sample of a
relevant literature but to provide a conceptual framework devised by the
author.   It will be through this process that the proposed study will be inserted into the continuing dialogue of scholarship within the domain of motor
development.

been suggested by Seigel (1969) and Austin
(1973) that improvement and gain of confidence through achievement in these attributes     **21**
may help to increase the self-concept of the
child and in so doing greatly enhance the
probability of success occurring in other
areas such as learning, communication, and
socialization.

Previous clinical studies by Johnson and Fretz
(1967), Fretz, Johnson, and Johnson (1969),
Cratty (1969), and Smith (1972) give support
that these types of clinics do aid in improv-     **22**
ing some aspects of perceptual-motor skill.
Studies by Falik (1969) and Goodman and Hammill
(1973) have, however, been critical as to the
effectiveness of the programs meeting their
objectives.

The attributes of perceptual-motor devel-     **23**
opment to be sutdied were arrived at by combining information obtained from factor analytic studies, a kinesio-perceptual study,
and other related literature (Fleishman, 1954;

**24**    Here, for the first time, the reader will see evidence that the author really means "perceptual *and* motor attributes" as separate categories rather than the generic category of "perceptual-motor" attributes.

Cratty, 1969; Sommers, Joiner, Holt, & Gross, 1970; Cratty, 1970; Geddes, 1972; Harrow, 1972). The attributes of strength, body part awareness, balance, gross agility, eye-hand coordination, power, and timing were the ones occurring most frequently or deemed most important in the literature. The perceptual attributes, ac- **24** cording to Cratty (1970), are those elements which are necessary for the acquisition of skill in the early stages. The motor factors, however, are those attributes such as reaction time, agility, and power which become more important in the later stages of skill development.

## PROCEDURES OF RESEARCH

### Selection of Subjects

This study will involve the population of children between the ages of seven and twelve who have been referred to the clinic by a variety of professional persons. The children all

**25**    The subjects appear to be quite heterogeneous with regard to condition, a fact that renders statistical analysis almost useless. Homogeneity of variance across treatment conditions and adequate sample size are the *sine qua non* of statistics. Here we have small samples of subjects who by clinical definition may be differentially incapable of responding to various aspects of the treatment.

**26**    Was the previous clinic from February to March of the previous year or from some more adjacent block of time? Performance on some of the proposed measures might be differentially influenced by a substantial interval between treatments. Timing tasks may reflect relatively permanent learning, whereas strength gains may dissipate. If there is to be a genuine distinction between groups one and two, there must be a reasonable presumption of a cumulative effect.

**27**    The treatments will be few, widely and unequally (in the case of absences) dispersed, a situation in which none but the most powerful intervention could reasonably be expected to produce noticable impact. This serious problem is too often found in graduate student research in physical education and is particularly characteristic of field studies. The time frame for typical degree programs at the masters level is inadequate for many investigations involving educational or therapeutic interventions as the independent variable. The consequence is not only a high probability for nonsignificance but an atmosphere of artificiality in which the research becomes an exercise rather than a genuine inquiry. Sensitivity of the measures employed is crucial whenever treatments are not robust. This matter might well be the subject of some discussion before the next draft of the proposal.

have some cluster of conditions involving **25**
perceptual-motor deficiency, poor social interaction skills, fitness deficits, and learning
and physical disabilities. There are to be
three groups participating in the study. The
first group will be those children who will
receive the clinic treatment but have also
attended the previous clinic program. The **26**
second group will also receive the clinic
treatment but will be attending for the first
time. The third group, which will serve as a
control, will be those children who are on a
"waiting list" for the next clinic. Group
one will involve approximately eight children.
The other two groups will each have fifteen
children.

Experimental Period

The clinical treatment will involve seven **27**
weekly sessions, each one hour in duration.
The clinic operates from early February until
late March. The children come every Saturday

**28** Some of the criteria as well as some of the terminology used in this paragraph are not consistent with the usual norms for analytical evaluation. For instance, it should be stated that the behavioral performances may be recorded on a ratio scale, that the tests have been shown to have high validity and objectivity coefficients, and that they produce normal and untruncated distributions of data. Tense shifts erratically within the paragraph.

morning from 10 to 11 a.m.  There will be a
make-up session at the end of the program for
any children who miss one of the Saturday
sessions.

## Dependent Variables

The tests to be used were obtained by meet-     **28**
ing several criteria.  All of the tests
(a) can be measured quantitatively and therefore have a high inter-observer reliability;
(b) do not produce a ceiling effect; (c) have
intra-test progression which is simple to
complex; (d) measure one of the perceptual-
motor attributes; (e) are available to the
practitioner in the field; (f) are easily
administered; and (g) have a strong theoretical basis.

Strength will be measured as the number of
kilograms obtained for right- and left-hand
grip strength tests.  A hand dynamometer will
be utilized (Sommers, Joiner, Holt, & Gross,
1970; Walker & Goslin, 1972).  Body part

**29**     If visual feedback is prevented in those children who balance 20 seconds, then
a second type of balance is being tested in some children but not in others.
Static balance with visual feedback is a totally different and independent
task, uncorrelated to static balance without visual feedback. This problem is
compounded and the results biased by selecting only those children who
achieve a certain level of performance to perform both of these tasks. The
reader must infer from this statement that the investigator has not read the
supportive literature relating to balance, nor has he formulated the theoretical basis upon which to select tests.

awareness will involve scoring points for

correctly identifying body parts of self and

of the tester (Cratty, 1969; Kephart, 1971).

Static balance will be measured as the number

of seconds the child balances on a 3-inch

square piece of wood on their preferred foot.

If the subject balances for 20 seconds then

a blindfold will be applied and the test re-    **29**

peated (Seefeldt, 1970; Sommers, Joiner, Holt,

& Gross, 1970).  In the dynamic balance test,

the distance covered in feet without falling

off the beam will be the score.  Different

width beams and the use of a blindfold will

be used for increasing complexity (Sommers,

Joiner, Holt, & Gross, 1970).  Gross agility

will be measured as the number of correct

movements executed in a floor pattern con-

sisting of 12 one-foot squares (Cratty, 1969).

Eye-hand coordination will be measured by the

number of seconds required to complete a test

involving the placement of two rows of ten

pennies in a box (Seefeldt, 1970).  Power

**30**   Validity and reliability figures for each test should be reported in the next draft, as should equipment specifications and a complete account of testing procedures (order of tests, test instructions, handling of children with physical disabilities, number of trials, scoring and recording procedures, etc.). If "tests and instrumentation" were placed in a category separate from "test administration," the reader would understand more clearly what is to take place.

**31**   Here is the nucleus of problems that characterize nearly all program evaluation studies undertaken by graduate students as thesis or dissertation research. A small number of available subjects, who possess a variety of unspecified but potentially relevant characteristics (in this case clinical, experiential, and developmental), are cast into treatment and control groups by non-random events, are then exposed to pre-treatment measures that are potentially reactive, and then subjected to short-term interventions that at best have been only broadly defined and are subject to no confirmatory control whatever. Construction of a careful link between the particulars of the treatment and the dependent variable is impossible from the outset. Given the small size and obvious heterogeneity of the groups, matching will not be a servicable tactic for design, nor will change scores be appropriate for the analysis. In the unlikely event that significant group differences are found, a host of lusty rival hypotheses will bid to account for the results.

   The design proposed here is the quasi-experimental model commonly called a "nonequivalent control group design." This design is defensible only to the extent that the groups involved are demonstrably equivalent (on all relevant dimensions). There is no apparent reason to believe this to be the case, and considerable presumptive evidence to suggest that it is not. In short, there is little or nothing that can be learned about the clinic's program through a design such as this. Even a set of carefully planned, sensitively executed, and measurement-supplemented case studies would yield far greater insight into the functioning of the program.

   Although it is not a function of this monograph to deal with research methods, there is a useful lesson to be drawn from the design problems confronted in this proposal. The researcher, in proposing these research tactics, is attempting to fit a square method into a round question. A traditional experimental format is applied to a problem that demands a unique set of empirical research tools. Such mismatching often has its genesis not in the student's naiveté, but in the circumstances of the graduate program. Available advisors in physical education generally have been prepared in experimental styles associated with the laboratory (whether in exercise physiology or motor learning). Few bring backgrounds in the behavioral sciences and fewer still in the complicated and dynamic area of educational or therapeutic program evaluation.

   Because of the attraction presented by the obvious practical implications of such studies, their often disarming surface simplicity, and the ease with which experimental designs can be mastered, many unwary students (and advisors) are lured into field studies involving program evaluation. Many of these studies have no possible chance of meeting basic standards of scientific acceptability. The lesson for the novice is clear. If you want to go into the field, find an advisor who knows the territory. Advisors who are at home in the laboratory may be lost in the school or clinic.

will be measured by the number of inches attained in a Sargent jump test. Timing will
be measured as the number of correct matchings
or reproductions of various rhythmical patterns involving hand and foot tapping
(Sommers, Joiner, Holt, & Gross, 1970).                    **30**

Design of the Study                                        **31**

All subjects in the three groups will be
tested on the previously mentioned perceptual-
motor attributes during the week before the
clinic commences and one week immediately
following the clinic program. This investigator and one research assistant will conduct
the testing. Initially, children will be en-
couraged to do their best, but no further
motivation will be given. The two experimental groups will then participate in a variety of gross motor activities, eye-hand
coordination skills, body image exercises,
relaxation and rhythmical activities, and
also games and modified sports during the

**32**    Exactly what this means is not clear.

clinic sessions. The testing apparatus will not be used in the clinic program. Each child has his/her own clinician and therefore receives attention on a 1:1 ratio. The clinician works by building on the strengths of the child while trying at the same time to improve the child's weaknesses. The program is very individual depending on the child's developmental level. The clinic also tries to work on a model of incorporating training of skills within a play atmosphere. Parents of the children are involved in discussions and talks since they are seen as a key in the support of their child at home. They meet with the clinicians and discuss ways of continuing the program at home. These are all important aspects in the total clinic treatment.

## Pilot Study

Before commencing with the testing design, the researcher will need to check his reli-

32

**33**    Pilot study work will be essential to judge the viability of the proposed study and thus should be completed prior to preparation of the final draft of the proposal.

**34**    It will be impossible to determine the status of each test with regard to each of the criteria through the use of small-scale pilot trials. For some items, the standardization literature will be the only recourse.

**35**    Reliability limits for acceptance or rejection of instruments should be pre-established and presented here with some sustaining rationale.

**36**    It should be clear by this point that the proposed experimental design is inadequate to answer the question posed in the study. Even if the design were appropriate, however, little information is provided in this section regarding the analysis. Many substantial questions remain unanswered:

a.    Is the pretest on all dependent variables, exclusive of treatment effects, correlated with the posttest? Will the experience of taking the pretest affect posttest performances? Is covariance a more viable analysis?

b.    What protections are available to account for the Hawthorne effect as a viable alternative hypothesis in this study? Also, the subjects in this study are particularly susceptible to the regression phenomenon. Should there not be a plan to analyze this?

c.    Is this a fixed effects or random effects model?

d.    What are the levels in the 3 x 2 analysis of variance?

e.    Is this a one between and one within fixed-effects model with three levels of the between factor and two levels of the within factor?

f.    What are the within-subject variances on each of the dependent variables?

g.    Should each variable be analyzed with a 3 x 2 analysis of variance model, or would a multivariate analysis better answer the question of the study?

h.    Will right- and left-hand strength scores be combined, or analyzed separately? How many strength trials and which of these trials will be used — first, last, average, or total?

i.    Will test reliabilities be established?

j.    Are the distributions normal for each of the dependent variables?

k.    How will the analyses be displayed?

ability of testing with a professional in the

field. A pilot study will be conducted with **33**

five children to ensure that each test item

satisfies the criteria by which it was se- **34**

lected. Since an assistant will be required

in the observation and recording of scores,

the pilot study will be used as part of his

training and also for establishing intra-

tester reliability. Test-retest reliability **35**

will also be obtained from the pilot study.

## Data Collection and Analysis

The data collected will be in the form of **36**

quantitative scores for each test. The scores

will be able to show differences for each sub-

ject on the pre- and post-treatment perform-

ance. A 3 x 2 analysis of variance will then

be used. A post hoc analysis of interaction

will be used to test the plausibility of rival

hypotheses which derive from the non-equiva-

lence of groups. Both individual as well as

group data will be used for analysis.

Since the literature is somewhat controversial, it will be hypothesized that there
will be no significant difference among groups.

BIBLIOGRAPHY

Austin, P. L.  The Role of Physical Education with Learning Disabilities, CAHPER Journal (in press), 1973.

Cratty, B. J. Perceptual and motor development in infants and children. London: The Macmillan Company, 1970.

Cratty, B. J., & Martin, Sister M. M. Perceptual-motor efficiency in children. Philadelphia: Lea and Febiger, 1969.

Espenshade, A. S., & Eckert, H. M. Motor development. Columbus, Ohio: Charles E. Merrill Publishing Co., 1967.

Falik, L. H. The effect of special perceptual-motor training in kindergarten on reading readiness and on second grade reading performance, Journal of Learning Disabilities, 1969, 2, 395.

Fleishman, E. A. Dimensional analysis of psychomotor abilities, Journal of Experimental Psychology, 1954, 48, 437.

Fretz, B. R., Johnson, W. R., & Johnson, J. A. Intellectual and perceptual-motor development as a function of therapeutic play, Research Quarterly, 1969, 40, 687.

Geddes, D. Factor analytic study of perceptual-motor attributes as measured by two test batteries, Perceptual and Motor Skills, 1972, 34, 227.

Goodman, L., & Hammill, D. The effectiveness of the Kephart-Getman activities in developing perceptual motor and cognitive skills, Focus on Exceptional Children, 1973, 4(9), 1-9.

Harrow, A. J. A taxonomy of the psychomotor domain. New York: David McKay Company, Inc., 1972.

Johnson, W. R. A humanistic dimension of physical education, Journal of Health, Physical Education, and Recreation, 1972 (November-December), 31.

Johnson, W. R., & Fretz, B. R. Changes in perceptual-motor skills after a children's developmental program, Perceptual and Motor Skills, 1967, 24, 610.

Kephart, N. C. The slow learner in the classroom. Columbus, Ohio: Charles E. Merrill Books, Inc., 1971.

Lord, J. C. Report on the children's developmental clinic. School of Physical Education, Dalhousie University, Halifax, Nova Scotia, December 1973.

Mann, L. Perceptual training: misdirection and directions, American Journal of Orthopsychiatry, 1970, 50, 30.

O'Connor, C. Effects of selected physical activities upon motor performance, perceptual performance and academic achievement of first graders, Perceptual and Motor Skills, 1969, 29, 703.

Pyfer, J. L., & Carlson, R. B. Characteristic motor development of children with learning disabilities, Perceptual and Motor Skills, 1972, 35, 291.

Seefeldt, V. Selected tests of perceptual motor behavior, in An introduction to measurement in physical education: Vol. 5, Laboratory manual of exercises, H. J. Montoye, Ed. Indianapolis: Phi Epsilon Kappa Fraternity, 1970.

Seigel, E. The real problem of minimal brain dysfunction, in Learning disabilities: its implications to a responsible society, D. Kronick, Ed. Chicago: Developmental Learning Materials, 1969.

Smith, M. C. Reversing reversals, Education and Training of the Mentally Retarded, 1972, 7, 93.

Sommers, P. A., Joiner, L. M., Holt, L. E., & Gross, J. C. Reaction time, agility, equilibrium, and kinesio-perceptual matching as predictors of intelligence, Perceptual and Motor Skills, 1970, 31, 460.

Walker, R. B., & Goslin, B. R. Physical efficiency laboratory manual. Department of Human Kinetics, University of Guelph, Guelph, 1972.

## PROPOSAL NUMBER 3
## INTRODUCTORY NOTE

This proposal represents an early-stage draft of a study involving the research tools of historiography. The term "prospectus" frequently is employed to designate a document used to try out a possible research topic before embarking on a full draft of the proposal. The intended audience may be a seminar group, a faculty committee, a research course instructor, a thesis advisor, or simply a group of available colleagues. The purpose is to sketch out a research problem with economy and clarity, a function well served by the outline format employed here. The question posed through use of this type of document is not "Is this a fully adequate plan for research?" but "Is this a researchable problem and does the author appear to be headed in the right general direction?"

**1**    The proposed title is terse, descriptive, and seems entirely appropriate to the problem.  One interesting consideration raised by the title, however, is that it appears to posit a conclusion before the research has been undertaken. It may be that in the student author's mind this particular point has been taken as an assumption, and is used in the title only as a way of describing the problematic territory.  Nevertheless, as indicated in the section of this monograph dealing with the "Scientific State of Mind," the problem of predetermined conclusions is a serious and sensitive one. Even though many readers would readily accept the proposition that the Games were a nationalistic endeavor and even though there is no intention to test that proposition in the proposed study, the inquiry does focus on the relationship between the Games and Jewish nationalism. For that reason it would be best to reformulate the title, even if the same elements are employed (example: Jewish Nationalism and the Maccabiah Games).

THE MACCABIAH GAMES:

A NATIONALISTIC ENDEAVOR   **1**


A Thesis Proposal


Presented to The

Supervising Committee

University of Erehwon


In Partial Fulfillment

of the Requirements for the Degree

Master of Education


by


A Graduate Student

October 1973

2    The author, not the study, will have to make the attempt.

THESIS PROSPECTUS

STUDENT'S NAME:  A Graduate Student

AREA OF SUBJECT MATTER:  History

CREDITS TO BE EARNED:  8

ADVISOR:  A Graduate Professor

I.  TITLE

The Maccabiah Games:  A Nationalistic
Endeavor

II.  STATEMENT OF THE PROBLEM

It is the purpose of this study to
examine some of the historical implications of Zionism and the growth of the
Maccabi World Union in its relationship
to the Maccabiah Games as a means of
Jewish nationalism.  This study will
attempt to answer the following ques-    2
tions:

(1)  What has been the historical relationship between Jews and their

**3**    Note that the question format used here seems more natural than the formal hypotheses employed in empirical research.

**4**    The last question shifts the frame of the study from the level of description and historical inquiry to a form of speculation, even prognostication, which will go beyond the ordinary uses of historical research. The reader may wonder whether at this point objective inquiry has shaded over into polemic. At the very least it would be appropriate to substitute "Has" for "Can." Many readers will fail to see any real distinction between the third and fourth questions. A careful reading of the definitions suggests that this is the case, unless the generic term "sport" extends the problem in some useful manner.

participation in sport?

(2) What is the relationship between **3**
Zionism and the Maccabi World
Union?

(3) Have the Maccabiah Games assisted
in carrying out the objectives
of Zionism?

(4) Can sport further Jewish nation- **4**
alism?

III. DEFINITION OF TERMS

The following terms are presented at
this time for general reference; more
detailed explanations will be given in
the study itself.

(1) Jew -- "A person descended, or
regarded as descended, from the
ancient Hebrews whose religion
is Judaism [Webster's New World
Dictionary, 1971, p. 297]."

(2) Maccabi World Union -- "International Jewish sports organi-

**5**     If the literature strongly supports this point (and the reader will suspect that
it does), then this point can be made as an assertion supported by direct evidence. Even if it is necessary to derive the conclusion from indirect evidence,
the reader will wonder why it is necessary to accept the proposition as a
fundamental prerequisite for the conduct of the study, which is the status
ordinarily accorded to basic assumptions. Perhaps the author felt obliged to
have an "assumption" of some kind, and this was the best of a bad lot.

zation ... [Encyclopaedia
Judaica, Vol. 11, 1971, p. 664]."

(3) Maccabiah Games -- "International
Jewish sports festival ... [Roth,
1962, p. 1241]."

(4) Nationalism -- "Loyalties based
upon a national ideal ... Common
aspirations, racial origin, home-
land, language, religion, and/or
culture ... [Van Dalen & Bennett,
1971, p. 199]."

(5) Zionism -- "The belief in the
existence of a common past and a
common future for the Jewish people [Laqueur, 1972, p. 589]."

IV. ASSUMPTIONS UNDERLYING THE RESEARCH

The investigation assumes that the　　5
formation of the Maccabi World Union by
the Zionist leaders in the early 1900's
was an attempt to unite Jewish youth.
The investigation further assumes that

**6**      The author has "assumed" these two points for the purpose of the investigation and is asking the reader to share the assumptions. Common usage in
everyday speech may make such personalizations as "the investigation assumes" commonplace, but in this context minor departures from strict form
often lead to less tolerable errors (see, for example, note 9 below). The
passive voice "it is assumed that . . . " provides clarity if not elegance.


**7**      The first two categories describing the scope of the study do not appear to be
similar, in nature or comprehensiveness, to the last category. The first two, if
taken to be attempts equal to the third, are overwhelming in their complexity
– each fully deserving as a thesis topic. If the phrase "attempt to define" is
taken literally, it places the first two categories in the position of being defined, whereas the third category consists of relationships to be established.
The author probably plans only to use a rather complete definition of the
first two categories as background information upon which to examine the
third category.

**8**      Removing the word "attempt" will remediate two problems. First it will remove the onus of effort from an abstraction ("the study") and place it where
it belongs. Second, the deletion will remove a needless provisional condition.
If nationalism cannot be defined as specified, there will be no study (at least
not in this form). The author fully intends to do it, not to attempt it. The use
of provisional conditions should be reserved for truly chancy operations (in
which case alternative courses of action should be described). The sentence
might properly begin "Nationalism will be defined . . . ."

**9**      A change to "The investigation will be limited . . ." would leave the author in
charge of things. Here the study seems to have gotten entirely out of hand.

the establishment of the Maccabiah    6
Games by the Maccabi World Union was a
further attempt to bring about Jewish
solidarity.

V.   SCOPE OF THE STUDY

This study will attempt to define    7
nationalism with respect to three cate-  8
gories:    (1) Nationalism in general;
(2) Nationalism specific in the Jewish
people; and (3) Nationalism and its relationship to sports.    This study will  9
limit its investigation of Zionism to
the relationship of the Zionist movement and sports.    The development, purpose, and achievements of the Maccabi
World Union will be presented as they
relate to the Maccabiah Games.    A description of the Games and their historical roots will be presented.    Finally, the accomplishments, implica-

**10**    A nice quotation but not helpful to the reader at this point; in fact, it detracts from the discussion of the real importance of the study. The proper use of quoted material is discussed in detail elsewhere in this monograph.

**11**    The word "attempt" simply is not necessary.

**12**    The material that follows does not provide what clearly has been promised. What "more" will the study provide? What will be added to knowledge that is not "descriptive" in nature? Such claims should be made with caution and backed with explicit plans for action.

tions, and future of the Maccabiah

Games will be discussed.

VI.    IMPORTANCE OF THE STUDY

Handlin (1954) states

> History is a method, a particular     **10**
> way, of studying the record of
> human experiences....the histor-
> ian endeavors to reconcile, clarify,
> and weave into a connected nar-
> rative the confusing happenings
> of the past [pp. 8, 9-10].

The Maccabiah Games have been called

a Jewish parallel to the modern Olympic

Games, but few people know of their ex-

istence.  Volumes have been written on

the modern version of the ancient Greek

games; numerous papers have been written

on the origins and development of these

games, but very few studies have con-

cerned themselves with the Maccabiah

Games and their origins.  This investi-      **11**

gation will attempt to present more than     **12**

a descriptive study of an international

sports festival.  It is the purpose of

**13**   A thesis such as the one proposed here would add (albeit modestly) to the store of human knowledge. To make it seem relevant only to "the profession" (physical education, one assumes) is unnecessarily parochial. If it is historical research done properly, the fact that sport is the focus need not limit the potential audience.

**14**   The phrase "Jewish sport" evokes the awkward picture of a special kind of sport. "Sport as participated in by Jews . . ." will better reflect what the author intends.

**15**   The abbreviated citation format is entirely appropriate to the functions of this preliminary document. The reader will want to know at this point only whether the student is aware of major sources, most of which are recognizable by the author's name or the title of the document. The categorization by subject area makes it easy to skim the material for major omissions. It might be useful at this stage to use a simple key to identify primary sources. In a study such as this, first-hand accounts will assume central importance.

this study to add to the knowledge of    **13**

the profession with regard to Jewish

sport and Jewish nationalism as achieved    **14**

through sport.


VII.    PROCEDURES

     A.    Preliminary steps to be pursued

        1. Literature review

| Nationalism | Maccabi World Union | **15** |
|---|---|---|
| Askin, 1966 | Bridger, 1962 | |
| Buber, 1963 | Gelber, 1946 | |
| Barlay, 1972 | Landman, 1948 | |
| Baron, 1971 | Roth, 1962 | |
| Jackson, 1966 | | |
| Janowsky, 1945 | Maccabiah Games -- Description | |
| Kohn, 1944 | | |
| Naamani, 1972 | Encyclopaedia Judaica, 1971 | |
| Schafer, 1972 | (The) Israeli Publishing In- | |
| Silvert, 1967 | stitute, 1969 | |
| Snyder, 1968 | Levine, date unknown | |
| Van Dalen & Bennett, 1971 | Muhlstein, 1973 | |

**16**     This section seems not properly to belong under a heading called "Steps to be Pursued." This may just have been an accident of hurried preparation, but more often such out-of-phase items are the result of feeling obliged to follow a prescribed outline format rather than the developing logic of the task at hand.

**17**     Aside from the question of placement, the opening sentence will provide a red flag for even the most casual reader. "This investigation will attempt to show . . . " is more than an amateurish slip of the tongue. It is dangerous language for any graduate student who expects to master the rudiments of science. The concern earlier expressed about the title and the issue of predetermined conclusions now is given fresh impetus. The student's misunderstanding here is fundamental. Research is not used to show or to prove anything. To do so moves the activity from research (which inquires as to what is) to advocacy (which argues for what ought to be). In the research process the nature of a relationship can be examined, but the process must be instructed by the nature of things, always holding open the possibilities that the relationship will assume unanticipated forms, or fail to appear at all.

What the author probably means is that one of the steps to be taken in the investigation is to search the literature for evidence that relationships exist among those items listed in 2(1). If this is the intention, then the type of evidence to be sought and the method to be used to find the evidence should be given in this section.

Newsweek Maga-
zine, 1973

Patai, 1971

Roth, 1962

Zionism

  Buber, 1973

  Buber, Magnes,
  & Simon, 1972

  Halpern, 1969 ,

  Laqueur, 1972

  Schneiderman &
  Karpman, 1965

  Selzer, 1970

  Sokolow, 1919

Maccabiah Games --
historical roots

  Ballou, 1970

Encyclopaedia
Judaica, 1971

Ehrlich, 1965

Friedman, 1969

(The) Holy
Scriptures, 1941

Josephus, date
unknown

Mezes, 1955

Postal, 1966

Roth, 1969

Siedentop, 1971

Toherikover, 1972

Vilnay, 1969

2. Specification of the problem **16**

This investigation will attempt **17**

to show a relationship between:

(1) The Zionist movement, the

Maccabi World Union, the

**18**     An alternative arrangement that might be more appropriate would be to place Section C, containing additional sources of information, here, adjacent to the list of background material to be employed in the preliminary review of literature. The section dealing with source criteria could then follow in natural order.

Maccabiah Games, and Jewish

nationalism.

(2) Sport and Jewish nation-            **18**

alism.

B.   Design of the study

1. Criteria for sources

The criteria for the selection

of sources for this study will

be based on the relevance of

the information found.   Primary

sources, whenever obtainable,

will be used.   The use of sec-

ondary sources will be to pro-

vide background information

relating to this investigation.

2. Criticism of the data

Criticism of the data will be

based primarily on the crite-

ria set forth by Van Dalen

(1973):

(1) Is the author accepted as
a competent observer and
reliable reporter?

**19**    For many readers there will be no immediate and clear distinction between
the two groups of source material: those listed for review in section A and
those suggested for search and subsequent review in section C. Is the distinction only that between what is at hand and what must be obtained by travel or
special loans? Or is one group mostly secondary whereas the other consists of
primary source material? Or is it a matter of the use intended for the materials; one group of references being employed in developing background concepts, such as the concept of nationalism, whereas the other is used to develop the main analysis, problems involving the Hebrew Union, Zionism, and
the Games. A clear-cut indication of the author's real intention here will help
the reader grasp the overall plan.

**20**    The list of potential sources is extensive and impressive. It will be difficult if
not impossible to accomplish much use of materials such as these without direct physical access. If visits to these resource centers are planned the reader
will want to know about it, even if such plans are only speculation at this
stage.

(2) Were his facilities, technical training, and loca-
tion favorable for observing the conditions reported?
(3) Did he report on direct observation, hearsay, or borrowed source materials?
(4) Did he write the document
at the time of the obser-
vation...?
(5) Did the author contradict
himself?
(6) Did the author distort or
embellish the truth to
achieve colorful literary
effects?
(7) Do accounts by other independent, competent obser-
vers ... agree with the
report of the author?
(p. 170)

C.  Plans for data gathering

1. Search for data                          19

Previously published and unpub-

lished materials relating to the

subject to be investigated will be

sought from: (1) The Maccabi World **20**

Union, Tel, Aviv, Israel, (2) Win-

gate Institute for Physical Education

and Sports, Dr. Stara Sherman acting

director, Netanya, Israel, (3) Israeli

Consulate, New York City.

**21**    Some indication of a proposed work schedule always is valuable. Particularly when travel appears to be essential, a proposed sequence for the search will reveal the degree to which priorities have been established and a desirable order for examining sources developed.

**22**    This sentence is ambiguous. What is a "re-evaluation of the problem"? How does such a process determine the relevance of data? This appears to be a case of inadequate written expression rather than defective planning.

(4) Jewish Museum of New York City,

(5) New York City Public Library,

(6) New York University Library,

(7) City College of New York Library,

(8) University of North Carolina at
Greensboro Library, (9) Hebrew Union
College, Cincinnati, Ohio, and (10)
Zionist Library and Archives,
New York.

2. Schedule for data gathering

Data will be gathered during    **21**
the 1974 Spring semester and Summer
sessions.

D. <u>Analysis</u>

1. Specification of techniques

The data obtained for this    **22**
investigation will be critically
examined and analyzed according to
its content. Re-evaluation of the
problem will be conducted to determine the relevance of the data
collected.

**23**    The chapter headings carefully reflect the series of questions posed on the first page of the prospectus. Reading the full range of topics to be covered, most experienced advisors will pause to reflect on the possibility that too much has been proposed — particularly for a masters thesis. In part, this is a subjective question that can be answered only in terms of the particular student involved. It is appropriate to note here, however, that the task laid out through Chapter IV is primarily one of putting together materials from primary sources into a cohesive and usable historical account of events. This is a reasonable, although still ambitious, undertaking. Although the tasks implied in the heading for the fifth chapter probably are intended to lend a sense of closure to the main questions, they also move the problem to a different and far more difficult level. Here the author has proposed to assemble evidence from a wide range of sources to develop a reasoned and empirically supported position about the real impact of the Games on Jewish nationalism. It is possible that the author already has assumed a position (a relationship of positive impact) and intends only to make some superficial assertions. This would be most regrettable, particularly if the descriptive work through Chapter IV was done thoroughly and competently. To develop a credible position sustained by sound scholarship might well constitute a subsequent study, perhaps a dissertation. Cutting a proposed project to appropriate size is a difficult and important task. The use of a prospectus such as this provides an early opportunity to begin discussion of that problem. A series of alternative plans may be spawned before the correct fit between task and available resources is obtained.

E. <u>Writing the report</u>

The proposed chapters and major **23**

headings will be:

I. Nationalism

    A. Definition

        1. general

        2. specific to the Jewish people

        3. relationship to sport

II. The Zionist Movement

    A. Description in relation to nationalism

    B. Relationship to sport

        1. objectives

        2. leaders and members

        3. accomplishments

        4. organizations

III. The Maccabi World Union

    A. As a nationalistic en-
deavor

    B. Objectives

    C. Accomplishments

IV. The Maccabiah Games

    A. Historical roots

    B. Description

        1. objectives

        2. guidelines for oper-
           ation

V. Achievements of the
Maccabiah Games

    A. Promotion of nationalism

    B. Implications for the future

        1. continuation of the
           games

# VII. PARTIAL BIBLIOGRAPHY

Aksin, B. States and nations. Garden City: Anchor Books, 1966.

Ballou, R. B., Jr. The role of the Jewish priesthood in the expansion of the Greek games in Jerusalem. First Canadian Symposium on Sport and Physical Education. University of Alberta, Edmonton, May 1970.

Barclay, G. Revolutions of our time, 20th century nationalism. New York: Praeger Publishers, 1972.

Baron, S.W. Modern nationalism and religion. Freeport: Books for Libraries Press, 1971.

Bridger, D. (Ed.) The new Jewish encyclopedia. New York: Behrman House, 1962.

Buber, M. Israel and the world. (2nd ed.) New York: Schocken Books, 1963.

Buber, M. On Zion, the history of an idea. New York: Schocken Books, 1973.

Buber, M., Magnes, J.L., & Zimon, E. (Ed.) Towards union in Palestine, essays on Zionism and Jewish-Arab cooperation. Westport, Conn.: Greenwood Press, 1972.

Ehrlich, E.L. A concise history of Israel. Translated by James Barr. New York: Harper Torchbook, 1965.

Encyclopaedia Judaica. Vol. 10. Jerusalem, Israel: Keter Publishing, 1971.

Encyclopaedia Judaica. Vol. 11. Jerusalem, Israel: Keter Publishing, 1971.

Encyclopaedia Judaica. Vol. 15. Jerusalem, Israel: Keter Publishing, 1971.

Friedman, E. Traditional and modern forms of physical education in the Bible and in modern Israel. Proceedings of the Sixth International Congress, Traditional and Modern Forms of Physical Education. Tokyo, Japan, August 1969.

Galber, N.M. Jewish life in Bulgaria. Jewish Social Studies, 1946, 8(2).

Gottschalk, L. Understanding history. New York: Alfred A. Knopf, 1950.

Gottschalk, L., Kluckhohn, C., & Angell, R. The use of personal documents in history, anthropology, and sociology. New York: Social Science Research Council, date unknown.

Halpern, B. The idea of the Jewish state. (2nd ed.) Cambridge, Mass.: Harvard University Press, 1969.

Handlin, O., Schlesinger, A.M., Morison, S.E., Merk, F., Schlesinger, A.M., Jr., & Buck, P.H. Harvard guide to American history. Cambridge, Mass.: Belknap Press, 1954.

(the) Holy Scriptures (according to the Masoretic text). Philadelphia: The Jewish Publication Society of America, 1941.

(the) Israeli Publishing Institute (Ed.). Great Jews in sports, the international Hebrew heritage library. Vol. 10. Miami: International Book Corporation, 1969.

Jackson, B.W. Nationalism and ideology. New York: W.W. Norton, 1966.

Janowsky, O.I. Nationalities and national minorities. New York: Macmillan Company, 1945.

Josephus, F. The works of Flavius Josephus. Vols. 1-3. Translated by William Whiston. New York: A.L. Burt, date unknown.

Kohn, H. The idea of nationalism, a study in its origins and background. New York: Macmillan Company, 1944.

Landman, I. (Ed.). The universal Jewish encyclopedia. Vol. 7. New York: Universal Encyclopedia Company, 1944.

Laqueur, W. A history of Zionism. New York: Holt, Rinehart & Winston, 1972.

Levine, H. Introduction. Unpublished manuscript, date unknown.

Mezes, A. The history of the Jews in ancient times. The Jewish people past and present. Vol. 1, New York: Jewish Encyclopedia Handbooks, 1955.

Muhlstein, J.M. Interview with David Pettruck, Unpublished manuscript, 1973.

Naamani, I.T. Israel, a profile. New York: Praeger Publishers, 1972.

Newsweek Magazine. An answer to Munich. 1973, 82, 65.

Patai, B. (Ed.) Sport and physical education in Israel. Encyclopedia of Zionism and Israel. New York: McGraw-Hill, 1971.

Postal, B. Biblical and Talmudic attitudes toward sports. Jewish Digest. 1966, 11(13), 49-54.

Roth, C. A short history of the Jewish people. (6th ed.) London: East and West Library, 1969.

Roth, C. (Ed.) The standard Jewish encyclopedia. Garden City: Doubleday, 1962.

Schafer, B.C. Faces of nationalism, new realities and old myths. New York: Harcourt, Brace, Jovanovich, 1972.

Schneiderman, H., & Karpman, I.J. (Ed.). Who's who in world Jewry, a biographical dictionary of outstanding Jews. New York: David McKay, 1965.

Selzer, M. (Ed.). Zionism reconsidered: the rejection of Jewish normalcy. New York: Macmillan Company, 1970.

Siedentop, D. Differences between Greek and Hebrew view of man. Canadian Journal of History of Sport and Physical Education. 1971, 2(2), 30-49.

Silvert, K.H. (Ed.) Expectant peoples, nationalism and development. New York: Vintage Books, 1967.

Snyder, L.L. The new nationalism. Ithaca: Cornell University Press, 1968.

Social Science Research Council. The social sciences in historical study. New York: Author, 1954.

Social Science Research Council. Theory and practice in historical study. New York: Author, 1946.

Sokolow, N. History of Zionism 1600-1918. London: Longmans, Green and Company, 1919. 2 vols.

Toherikover, U. The Hellenistic movement in Jerusalem and Antiochus' persecutions. In A. Schalitt (Ed.), The World history of the Jewish people, the Hellenistic age. New Brunswick: Rutgers University, Jewish History Publications, 1972.

Van Dalen, D.B. Understanding educational research. New York: McGraw-Hill, 1973.

Van Dalen, D.B., & Bennett, B.L. A world
   history of physical education. (2nd ed.)
   Englewood Cliffs: Prentice-Hall, 1971.

Vilnay, Z. Sport in ancient Israel. Proceedings of the First International Seminar on the History of Physical Education
   and Sport. Netanya, Israel, April 1968.

Webster's new world dictionary of the
   American language. (pocket-sized ed.)
   New York: Popular Library, 1971.

# Appendix A
# Some General Standards
# for Judging
# the Acceptability of a Thesis
# or Dissertation Proposal

## Some General Standards for Judging the Acceptability of a Thesis or Dissertation Proposal

| | Desirable | Undesirable |
|---|---|---|
| **I. Topic**<br>**A. Importance**<br>**1. Basic Research** | Topic is articulated to a body of knowledge recognized as broadly relevant to professional concerns. There is a clear relation between the topic and existing information in related areas of knowledge. Topic is recognized as substantial by people who are knowledgeable in the area. | Proposal does not support the importance of the study. Topic seems unrelated to existing facts and theoretical constructs. Proposed study is not inserted into a line of inquiry. |
| **2. Applied Research** | Topic is relevant to professional needs, and recognized as substantial by competent individuals engaged in professional practice. There is a clear relation between the topic and existing problems in practice. | Topic seems unrelated to realistic professional concerns and divorced from matters of practice. |
| **B. Scope** | The extent of the proposed study is reasonable in terms of the time and resources available to the candidate. There is clear indication that the student has considered and made provision for each of the demands implicit within the study. | Projected study is grandiose and unreasonable in terms of time and resources. Or, the study is so small or limited in its concern as to provide little useful information and to involve less than a reasonable exposure to scholarly inquiry for the candidate. |

| | Desirable | Undesirable |
|---|---|---|
| C. Advisement | At least one faculty member possessing scholarly competence in the domain of the topic is both interested and available. Resources for developing or obtaining needed technical skills are available and specifically identified. | Faculty members available for substantial assistance lack special competence in the domain of the topic. Needed sources of technical assistance are not specified or identified. |
| II. Scholarship<br>A. Originality | The proposal provides in the definition of the problem, the methodology employed, or the mode of interpretation, some contribution that is different from work previously done, and that distinctly is the product of the candidate's own thinking. In replicative studies special attention is given either to deliberate alteration in method and design or to the unique problems of maintaining equivalent conditions for all critical variables. | Proposed study paraphrases and collects opinions, results, or conclusions of others without criticism, synthesis, or the creative development of an organizing structure. Replicates without intentional and appropriate variation in method or special attention to the problems of creating a satisfactory level of experimental equivalence. |
| B. Perspective | Student reveals that he is able to relate his topic to a larger framework of knowledge and theory. | Student treats the problem in isolation from previous work, related disciplines, and relevant theoretical structures. |
| C. Logic | Design of the proposed study is appropriate to the nature of the topic, being no more elaborate than demanded by the question | Proposed design is more complex than demanded by the question and the present level of knowledge. Design fails to confront im- |

| | Desirable | Undesirable |
|---|---|---|
| | asked. There is congruence among title, problem, and procedures. Student makes explicit the rationale and assumptions that underlie the form of the question and the procedures selected. He reveals alternatives that might have been followed and makes visible the reasoning for his choices. | portant complexities in the topic through the use of methods leading to multivariate analysis. Title does not exactly reflect the central problem. Procedures are not designed to deal with the problem identified as central to the study. Student does not make clear the procedural alternatives that might have been followed. |
| D. Objectivity | Student clearly delineates the limits, weaknesses, and strengths of his study, and maintains objectivity. He restricts his language to a level made justifiable by previous findings and a conservative appraisal of current knowledge and practice. | Student overgeneralizes from an inadequate body of knowledge or suggests applications that seem unwarranted by the evidence he presents. He seems unaware of the limitations imposed by his selection of sample or methodology. |
| E. Depth of Preparation | Student demonstrates familiarity with the major sources of information that relate to his problem, and makes apt and ready application of these to the development of his study. Includes pilot study data, power tests for determining sample size, and relevant sample applications of the methods to be employed. Student makes clear that he has considered the feasibility factors of time, | Student has not completed a thorough search of relevant literature, or has not digested it to the point of understanding the major concepts involved and their application to his problem. Proposal includes no pilot study data or relevant sample applications of methods to be employed. He fails to recognize the sophisticated scholarship needed for the use of such procedures as sampling, use of demographic |

| | Desirable | Undesirable |
|---|---|---|
| III. Presentation | | |
| A. Mechanics | Proposal is well edited, with adequate attention to grammar, sentence structure, spelling, and all matters of mechanical accuracy. The style is terse, with a minimum of unnecessary words and irrelevant commentary. | cost, and the availability of data. Student indicates how he plans to obtain special competencies demanded by his procedures.<br><br>Obvious failure to proofread as revealed by mechanical errors. Unnecessary use of descriptive words and phrases. Rambling style, introduction of peripheral commentary, and use of trite jargon. |
| B. Documentation | Citations are limited to and consistently provided for (a) concepts, procedures, or materials (including quoted materials) that are the unique products of particular individuals and fall under the broad canon of "credit due" and (b) positions, interpretations, or methodological alternatives elected by the author that might require the support of further argument and explication as developed in supplementary references. | Inadequate reference to the relevant literature, failure to give credit where due, or failure to indicate sources likely to be needed by the interested and critical reader. Overabundance of documentation in which citations are irrelevant, needlessly repetitious, or refer to matters clearly within the public domain. Extensive use of direct quotations that are not justified by their contribution to the main tasks of the proposal. |
| C. Organization | Proposal has logical, easily understandable sequence from initial statement of the problem through last appendix. Major topics are separated under appropriately | Order of topics violates logic and causes reader to skip forward and back to make sense of the presentation. Words used to indicate systematic meanings, prior to their |

| | Desirable | Undesirable |
|---|---|---|
| D. Clarity | devised sub-headings. Format tailored to meet demands peculiar to the topic. Proposal makes explicit each step of the project. Procedures are described in terms of specific operations. Copies of such relevant materials as test instruments, interview schedules, directions to subjects, criteria for selection of experts, and pilot test data are appended to the main proposal document. Given the level of detail contained in the proposal, any appropriately trained researcher could carry out the study with results not differing substantially from those that would be obtained by the author. Explicit, step-by-step sequence of operations presented. | definition. Arbitrary format followed even when inappropriate to topic. Report makes vague references to unspecified procedures that are described only in general terms or that are linked together by relationships that leave their purpose unclear. Such important operations as "a structured interview," "an analysis of literature," "an evaluation of materials," or "a test of attitudes" are not presented in explicit forms such as particular test instruments, lists of criteria, procedures for analysis, or experimental operations. Exact temporal sequence of individual parts of the investigation not made clear. |

# Appendix B
# Annotated Bibliography of
# Supplementary References

## INTRODUCTION

Few published documents have focused specific attention on the preparation of research proposals. Davitz and Davitz (6),* Crawford and Kielsmeier (5), and Krathwohl (13) are among the rare exceptions to this rule. The great bulk of written advice available to the novice researcher will be found in two kinds of sources; in both the authors give primary attention to other tasks. First are textbooks about research, which deal largely with the methodology of performing research. Second are the instruments developed to be used in evaluating the adequacy of reported research. These instruments deal, ex post facto, with the products of proposals.

Only rarely have the authors of research evaluation instruments suggested that such tools might be used with profit at the planning stage. It has always been more attractive (among senior educational researchers at least) to attack the relatively pure and abstract problems of distinguishing between adequate and inadequate research reports than to become involved in the concrete and often convoluted struggle to find appropriate strategies before the research is performed. In research as in other human enterprises the exercise of hind-

---

*Numbers indicate items in the annotated bibliography.

sight is far more popular than the uncertain task of achieving foresight. The industrious novice will discover, however, that evaluation instruments designed to treat research reports are an excellent source of ideas for critical analysis at many stages of proposal development.

In this brief set of annotations we make no attempt to exhaust any category of useful resources. Included below are items that we have found useful in helping students and ourselves create better research proposals. For the most part we have selected readily obtainable inexpensive paperbacks that can form the basis of a small reference shelf for the graduate student.

Readers interested in a more extensive list of materials devoted to the evaluation of research should see Bartos (2) and Hodges (11) below. No attempt has been made to include more than a sampling of traditional research method textbooks. Students will soon discover the standard references that are most useful for the particular form and subject emphasis of their own research. For example, D. R. Cox's *Planning of experiments* has long been a staple for graduate students proposing experimental research involving psychological variables, and E. F. Lindquist's *Design and analysis of experiments in psychology and education* is an almost universal resource in articulating statistical analysis to study design. At the time of this writing all the resources noted below are still in print or are available through the indicated sources.

1. **Allen, G. R.** *The graduate students' guide to theses and dissertations.* **San Francisco: Jossey-Bass Publishers, 1973.**

This book was prepared expressly for graduate students confronted with a research requirement as part of their degree program. Brisk, systematic, entirely non-technical in language and completely practical in approach, this popular manual makes an excellent starting place from which to obtain an overview of the entire graduate research process.

Each chapter is constructed around commonly asked questions (with appropriate answers) concerning the task of completing graduate theses and dissertations. The text divides the research process into seven steps, some of which follow the traditional format ("collecting data") whereas others involve topics less frequently given public discussion ("getting a committee" and "defending your research").

Special attention is given throughout to the fact that students will be confronted with a variety of rules and traditions peculiar to their own institutions. A list of questions following each chapter is designed to help students identify how the general rules provided in the text must be adapted to meet the demands of their own local situation.

The brief chapter on preparing research proposals provides only a superficial overview of that central task. Other chapters, however, such as "Selecting a Research Topic" and "Writing the Research Report," offer much greater detail and include a number of novel insights that should be helpful to the beginner in research. The chapter dealing with data collection contains a particularly strong section on the design and use of questionnaires. Emphasis on the decisions and events that occur before and after the preparation of the proposal make Professor Allen's book an excellent supplement to the present text.

2. **Bartos, B. B.** *A review of instruments developed to be used in the evaluation of the adequacy of reported research* **(Phi Delta Kappa Research Service Center Occasional Paper No. 2). Bloomington, Indiana: Phi Delta Kappa, 1969.**

In addition to a brief review of research evaluation procedures, this small booklet contains a listing of 42 checklists and rating instruments for the evaluation of research. Although the instruments cover a wide range of types, sophistication, focus, and utility, nearly all of them may be used with profit in the process of evaluating proposals. Many of the items have been published or are available through sources such as interlibrary loan, ERIC, or University Microfilms. A graduate department might collect and maintain a file containing those instruments that prove to be particularly useful for student researchers.

3. **Campbell, D. T., and Stanley, J. C.** *Experimental and quasi-experimental designs for research.* **Chicago: Rand McNally Co., 1963.**

Although this is ordinarily thought of as a treatise on research design (certainly it is one of the most lucid treatments of design ever produced for a broad readership), the authors of this elegant monograph have so much to say about the broad standards of systematic inquiry that it should be consumed by every graduate student at an early point in his or her research preparation. Building around the format provided by a theoretical model of validity for inquiry, the authors examine 16 different designs for research and a host of vital issues that touch the preparation of sound proposals.

4. **Cook, D. R.** *A guide to educational research.* **Boston: Allyn and Bacon, 1965.**

This unique paperback is intended for the beginning graduate student in a research method course at the masters degree level. The heart of the book is not the discussion of methods (chapters are devoted to historical, descriptive, and experimental research), but the ten reports that are subject to analysis. Each study is bracketed by an introduction and an analysis prepared by the author. Although method and interpretation of results occupy a substantial portion of the commentary, some valuable discussion is devoted to the form and logic of presentation. These matters apply as much to the proposal as to the report. Two useful chapters conclude the book with advice on defining the research question and preparing the proposal.

5. **Crawford, J., and Kielsmeier, C.** *Proposal writing.* **Corvallis, Oregon: Continuing Education Publications, 1970.**

This well-produced and relatively large (169 pages) volume is a solid value. Intended both as a learning tool and as a working reference for educators interested in designing their own research projects, the book employs the style (and occasionally the format) of a programmed learning textbook.

Part I contains a brief, nontechnical orientation to the central concepts in proposal writing. Written in a breezy, informal style, the text employs a graphic "how to do it and what to avoid" approach of a true manual or handbook. Part II contains appendices relevant to use of the manual. These include annotated bibliographies related to each of the main components of proposal writing, a list of funding sources, and two specimen proposals.

The workbook section itself (Part III) approaches proposal writing as a series of specific cognitive skills. The skills needed for writing experimental research proposals and those needed for writing development project proposals are presented in alternating order throughout the workbook. Thirteen major components of the proposal are identified; discussion, examples, and competence exercises are provided for each.

Part IV (Evaluating Proposals) contains the HEW Guidelines for proposal evaluation as well as a copy of the Field Reader's Evaluation Form. Evaluations employing the HEW format are provided by several Field Readers for each of two proposals reprinted in this section (one for experimental research and one for a developmental program). This makes it possible for a student using the text to employ the HEW form to evaluate the proposals and then compare their conclusions with those of expert reviewers.

It is difficult to imagine a more useful text for the graduate student facing the preparation of a first proposal. For the investment of several surprisingly painless evenings the student should achieve a refocusing of otherwise abstract and disparate learning experiences in statistics, design, and measurement, on the practical problem of writing a plan for research. Copies may be obtained from Continuing Education Publications, 100 Waldo Hall, Corvallis, Oregon 97331.

6. **Davitz, J. R., and Davitz, L. J.** *A guide for evaluating research plans in psychology and education.* **New York: Teachers College Press, 1967.**

This inexpensive 38-page paperbound monograph includes both discussion of the problems encountered in preparing a proposal and an excellent checklist for the evaluation of such research plans. Written entirely in nontechnical language, the text gives clear and always precise treatment to a wide range of research considerations. If a book has ever been written about research that one could read simply for pleasure, this graceful little monograph must be it. The checklist contains 25 major problem areas common to proposal development. By posing critical questions, the text provides standards for each of the problem areas. Questions are followed in each case by a discussion of practical considerations in formulating the strongest possible plan for action.

7.   **Educational Innovators Press.** *Critiquing a proposal.* **Tucson, Arizona: Educational Innovators Press, 1968.**

This 25-page booklet is part of a series of instructional and practice materials designed to prepare educators with the skills necessary to propose and evaluate a variety of innovative school programs. Included here are five short research proposals, a simple rating system, and an answer list. The booklet is intended for use in an instructional setting and requires supplementation through discussion and other resource materials. Although the evaluation system itself will be of little use, the novice will find the proposals (complete with obvious defects) useful reading. The research design diagrams are particularly good. The terse format used for these mini-proposals can well be copied by students in sketching out preliminary proposal drafts.

8.   **Gephart, W. J.** *Profiling educational research* **(Phi Delta Kappa Research Service Center Occasional Paper No. 3). Bloomington, Indiana: Phi Delta Kappa, 1969.**

See the annotation for Gephart and Bartos (9) below. This is the original scholarly paper from which the instructional package was later produced. This booklet contains all the tabular materials and flow charts used in the profiling system plus a brief discussion of the evaluation procedure.

9.   **Gephart, W. J., and Bartos, B. B.** *Profiling instructional package* **(Phi Delta Kappa Research Service Center Occasional Paper No. 7). Bloomington, Indiana: Phi Delta Kappa, 1969.**

This 47-page booklet undertakes what must be the most ambitious instructional task ever attempted in research education – to provide a set of instructions and a system of evaluation so carefully prepared that an intelligent lay person can evaluate empirical research. Whether a reader who does not initially know the difference between a median and a mode can actually determine whether a given analysis demands a Friedman Two-Way Anova or a Mahalanobis $D^2$ is open to some question. There is no question, however, about the qualitative excellence of the instructional package.

The profiling system deals only with methodological adequacy. As this is taken to include such sophisticated considerations as the internal logic of the hypotheses and the existence of rival hypotheses, in addition to the more obvious topics of sampling, treatment, measurement, and data analysis, the coverage provides much that is relevant to the early stages of research planning.

Fold-out flow charts and careful instructions make it possible for the novice to practice the skills of logical research analysis in tidy, step-by-step order. Definitions are terse and lucid with simple examples inserted at difficult junctures. Although they are derived from previous efforts, the three charts used to identify appropriate methods of statistical analysis for any given set of data are in themselves worth the price of purchase. Advanced graduate students with a stronger background in statistics will find it instructive to expand and revise these useful charts.

By profiling the quality of research reports (on ordinal scales), the authors make explicit the limitations and tradeoffs that characterize nearly all educational research. The central concept of qualitative profiling for five separate areas of the research plan is particularly helpful in the area of physical education, where there has been much confusion about the utility or even propriety of relative rather than absolute standards for research evaluation.

As an exercise in research education, or as a pony for use in reviewing their own proposal efforts, novice researchers in physical education can profit from this excellent if still imperfect attempt to devise the "perfect" evaluation system.

10. Hall, M. *Developing skills in proposal writing* (Office of Federal Relations, Oregon State System of Higher Education). Corvallis, Oregon: Continuing Education Publications, 1971.

This 194-page paperbound document is directed to the needs of individuals preparing sponsored project and grant applications to agencies of the federal government. The primary orientation is to proposals dealing with training, demonstration, and service programs rather than with research activities. A companion publication (see item 5) deals more closely with application for federal funding of research.

Four chapters deal directly with the task of writing the proposal. Typically couched in a series of "do" and "don't" guidelines, the overall effect of the text is one of terse, graphic, thorough, and completely knowledgeable advice from a battle-hardened insider. Sample application forms and case studies of successful proposals are included in profusion.

Chapter 9, dealing with evaluation, is particularly useful to students considering research proposals involving program or clinic evaluation in the field. Strategies for evaluation, selection of measuring instruments, and data collection procedures are given close attention.

The text has the special advantage of field testing in a variety of educational settings, with subsequent revisions to incorporate suggestions arising from that process. In addition to its considerable utility as a writing guide, the book is valuable as a practical outline of procedures to use in obtaining funds for the support of scholarship, a matter of obvious importance in all research.

11. Hodges, C. S. *Measuring educational research quality and its correlates.* New York: Columbia University, Bureau of Applied Social Research, 1967.

Initially prepared as a masters thesis, this document reports a research project designed to develop an instrument to measure the quality of educational research. Also included is a field application of the instrument in testing several theories concerning the nature of educational research. The extensive appendices contain full copies of several other rating instruments and instructions for their use. Included are instruments devised by David Nasatir, William Gephart, and Sam Sieber.

The second revision (1966) of the Nasatir instrument provides a rating scale with objectified criteria and standards established over a range of qualitative levels. This six-page rating system is particularly appropriate for many forms of physical education research and represents one of the best tools available among the shorter instruments. As with many of the evaluation schemes, the user must bring considerable research expertise to the process of applying such instruments. Nevertheless, the novice can profit by noting the issues raised, even if he is unsure of their appropriate resolution.

The full, unpublished thesis is available on interlibrary loan from the Columbia University Library for a fee. The Library will provide a Xerox copy at a page rate plus postage. A copy of the report prepared for the sponsoring agency (not in thesis format) may be borrowed from the Bureau of Applied Social Research at 605-7 West 115th St., New York, New York 10027, by sending a refundable deposit.

12. Hubbard, A. W. (Ed.). *Research methods in health, physical education and recreation* (3rd revised edition). Washington, D.C.: American Association for HPER, 1973.

Nearly every graduate student in physical education will encounter this text at some time in the process of obtaining an advanced degree. A collection of separately authored sections of varying quality and intelligibility, there are four chapters worthy of the novice's attention prior to the selection of a research topic: Chapter 2 by Benjamin Massey (Overview of Research: Basic Principles), Chapter 3 by Marion Broer and Dorothy Mohr (Selecting and Defining a Research Problem), Chapter 4 by Vern Seefeldt (Searching the Literature), and Chapter 14 by Hope Smith (Writing Proposals, Theses, Dissertations, Research Articles).

The authors in this AAHPER-sponsored collection sometimes take positions and offer advice that are at considerable variance with what has been espoused in this present monograph. Wise students will contrast and weigh the differing points of view and make a choice that best fits their circumstance and personal predilection.

13.  **Krathwohl, David R.** *How to prepare a research proposal.* **Syracuse, New York: Syracuse University Bookstore, 1965.**

In 50 concise pages Krathwohl reveals a multitude of considerations that must be confronted prior to the formulation of a proposal for the funding of a research project. This monograph is similar to others on the topic in that it provides suggestions for writing the proposal sections: problem statement, related research, objectives, procedures, design, and facilities. It differs from others in that the suggestions are pertinent to researchers who seek financial support from the United States Office of Education specifically, and from other governmental agencies generally. It also provides practical information helpful to solving the nettlesome problems of constructing a budget, explaining personnel to be used, and developing a workable time-frame for the project. Suggestions are made for writing an abstract of the proposed study.

The table of contents serves the dual purpose of organizing the content as well as of providing a checklist with which the reader may analyze a proposal's strengths and weaknesses. An appendix includes suggested modifications for proposed survey studies, predictive studies, methodological studies, equipment, instrument and material development studies, philosophical and historical studies, and longitudinal studies.

Another unique section is the discussion of characteristics of the granting agency. Knowledge about the scope of the grant program as well as the review process used by the granting agency is of obvious value in the construction of a proposal, yet authors of texts related to the subject rarely discuss these important aspects of proposal writing.

This monograph will be valuable to anyone about to write a proposal for research. Krathwohl has required his graduate students to write their thesis proposals as though they were proposing their project for funding from a granting agency. He suggests that this practice provides experience in writing proposals, but also encourages the student to move quickly toward realistic plans by demanding that they plan their time and budgets. The *coupe de maître* is that several of his students' research projects have indeed been funded! The monograph may be obtained at a modest price from Syracuse University Bookstore, 303 University Place, Syracuse, New York 13201.

14. Kroll, W. P. *Perspectives in physical education.* New York: Academic Press, 1971.

This textbook is a combination of history, status report, critical analysis, and personal polemic, all concerning the research enterprises of physical education. Aside from the importance of the book as a position statement by one of the profession's foremost research scholars, it provides several chapters specifically designed for the novice researcher confronting the proposal task. Of particular value are Chapter 10 (Establishing Priorities in Research), which treats a vital topic not touched upon here, and Chapter 11 (Writing Up Research), which contains a number of practical suggestions for the preparation of a sound proposal document.

15. Leedy, Paul D. *Practical research: planning and design.* New York: Macmillan, 1974.

Although not a programmed text, this paperbound manual is something of a do-it-yourself guide. The central four chapters are devoted to design; the remaining chapters all pertain to the problems of planning and reporting. A full-scale proposal is reprinted in the appendix, complete with a running critical commentary by the author. Although some of the commentary on the specimen proposal deals with design and methodology and some of the standards for proposal preparation diverge sharply from those espoused by the present authors, the overall intention runs closely parallel to this monograph.

A second appendix provides a thoughtfully devised set of ten exercises (called "projects") for use by graduate students preparing for a research task. Among the projects is the use of an evaluation procedure for rating research reports. A brief checklist of evaluative standards is provided. The system can easily be converted to deal with proposals rather than reports.

Close attention to scores of minor details makes this text an invaluable aid in the practical business of producing a written document. Written in a crisp, lucid prose style, and produced in a graphic, easy-to-use format, this book will meet the needs of many students for a self-instruction reference to supplement work in classes and seminars.

16. Massengale, John D. *The research proposal in physical education.* Cheney, Washington: DJ Publishing Co., 1972 (Rt. 3, Box 19, Cheney, Washington).

This inexpensive, privately published booklet (70 pages) provides a brief overview of the major elements in the proposal. Designed explicitly for the novice in physical education, the two major chapters deal with such fundamental matters as topic selection, the use of style manuals, and topical sections within the traditional proposal format. Although it is not subject to critical analysis by the author, a full-scale specimen proposal is included in the appendix. The booklet might serve as a useful supplementary text in introductory courses dealing with research at the upper division or masters level. Several sections from the book have appeared in *The Physical Educator* in recent years.

17. **Mouly, G. J.** *The science of educational research.* **New York: American Book, 1963.**

Although it has been less popular than some others, this introductory level textbook is a typical example of the genre. We include it here less because of its particular importance than because physical education students should be aware that most university libraries contain entire shelves of such resource books, some of which can be most helpful in dealing with particular problems in research planning.

The treatment of methodology necessarily is simplistic, but two chapters will have utility for the graduate student embarking on a first proposal. Chapter 14 (Educational Research: A Review and Evaluation) outlines a number of pitfalls peculiar to educational research. Chapter 16 (The Thesis and Dissertation) contains some common-sense advice concerning the mechanics of research writing.

18. **Solley, W. H. A check list for adequacy of experimental research involving human performance.** *The Physical Educator,* **1966, 26, 165-166.**

This check list evaluation form is intended specifically for use at the proposal stage and is directed toward experimental research in physical education. Reprinted and variously reworked versions of this instrument have circulated through physical education departments for many years. In the process these versions often lose the citation crediting Solley with authorship of this small but important contribution to our research literature. The major advantage of the instrument is its brevity and breadth of coverage. By the same token, it lacks objectified criteria and any attention to rating relative levels of success in meeting abstract standards of adequacy. The list includes consideration of problem selection, proposal organization and preparation, procedures, analysis of data, and general scholarship.

A useful exercise for the novice researcher is to prepare objectified (behaviorized) descriptions of proposal components, in each of Solley's rating areas, at four levels of adequacy (perhaps: inadequate, minimal, satisfactory, and superior). Having accomplished this, the student not only will have a proposal evaluation instrument of much greater utility than Solley's original, but more than a little insurance against failing to recognize inadequacies in his own proposal.

**19.** **Stephens, J. M. Making dependable use of published research: a proposed check list.** *The Journal of Educational Research,* **1967,** *61,* **99-104.**

The author proposes an ingenious check list and flow chart designed to force the neophyte researcher into an objective interpretation of the results of experimental investigation. The check list is limited to use only with experimental studies that deal with questions of causality, and it is designed for the consumer of research rather than the proposer of research.

The advantages of using the check list are that it provides an orderly and efficient sequence of questions to be asked to reduce the likelihood of erroneously accepting conclusions that have not been supported by the data. In addition, it reminds the less experienced researcher of flaws that might be overlooked and encourages him to construct rival hypotheses that would lead him to be critical about accepting a proposed conclusion.

Although the check list is designed for the consumer of research, a meticulous proposer of research might find it to be a valuable tool in predicting unwanted alternative hypotheses. Its purpose is to force the interpreter into a cold, mechanistic, objective procedural analysis of alternative hypotheses to explain the research results. If the proposer of research assumed that the results of his proposed study verified the stated hypotheses, the checklist might reveal alternative hypotheses that could, with further experimental control, be eliminated.

# Appendix C
# Standards for the Use
# of Human Subjects
# and Specimen Form
# for Informed Consent

The following guidelines were developed for use in classes that require students to conduct original investigations involving human subjects.

## GUIDELINES FOR STUDENT-CONDUCTED
## STUDIES INVOLVING SUBJECTS DRAWN
## FROM UNIVERSITY CLASSES

These guidelines presume investigations in which the procedures offer no risk to the welfare of the subjects. Any investigation involving physical or psychological risk to the subject falls under the University regulations governing the Welfare of Human Subjects. Full proposals for all such investigations must be submitted to and approved by the appropriate University committees.

Each student who undertakes an investigation involving human subjects as part of course requirements and who wishes to utilize subjects in any regularly scheduled University course must plan and execute his investigation in such manner as to conform to each of the following guidelines.

1.  Consent must be obtained from the course instructor(s) involved. This must include a discussion of dates on which student subjects

will be needed, the time involved, the exact demands to be placed on subjects, and all relevant details of the investigation.

2.  All subjects used must be volunteers who freely give their cooperation without coercion of any kind. Further, it shall be made clear by both the investigator and the regular course instructor that grades for the course are entirely unaffected by participation (or non-participation) in the investigation.

3.  Every effort must be exerted to minimize interruption of regular instruction. Subjects must be removed quietly and expediently from the class and returned promptly after each use. The physical site of the investigation must be planned so as to present a minimum of interruption or distraction to ongoing class work.

4.  No subject may be removed from class for a total period of treatment time exceeding 10% of the available instructional time during any one semester.

5.  All subjects shall be informed of the nature of the investigation, including the basic purpose and the exact form of all procedures. Whenever it is necessary to withhold any item of information concerning purpose or procedure, provision will be made for the prompt and thorough debriefing of all subjects.

6.  An "informed consent" form will be drawn up by the investigator (see attached specimen showing the suggested format) and approved by the sponsoring faculty member. Each subject must read and sign an individual consent form. Completed consent forms must be filed with the sponsoring professor.

7.  All subjects must be informed that they are free to withdraw their consent and terminate participation at any time.

8.  All subjects must be offered an opportunity to learn the results of the study. Every effort must be exerted to maintain the interest and good will of the subjects with regard to participation in University sponsored research.

9.  Although not normally subject to University regulations governing the welfare of human subjects, each investigator must read the University policy as it appears in the *Faculty Handbook*. Each investigator will be held accountable for behavior in full accord with the standards set forth in those regulations.

## SPECIMEN: SUGGESTED FORMAT FOR CONSENT FORM.

### INFORMED CONSENT

I understand that the purpose of this study is to learn more about . . . .

I confirm that my participation as a subject is entirely voluntary. No coercion of any kind has been used to obtain my cooperation.

I understand that I may withdraw my consent and terminate my participation at any time during the investigation.

I have been informed of the procedures that will be used in the study and understand what will be required of me as a subject.

I understand that all of my responses, written or oral, will remain completely anonymous.

I wish to give my cooperation as a subject.

*Signed:* _____